WHO AM I?

Endorsements

VERA'S POETRY MEMOIR book offers a uniquely intimate and powerful reading experience, weaving together the raw emotion of lived experiences of herself and her family with the lyrical beauty of verse. Unlike traditional memoirs, the poetic form allows her to distill memory, trauma, joy, and transformation into moments of pure, resonant language and invites the reader not just to understand, but to feel. Opportunities for the reader to contemplate and discover what they believe and think, create teachable moments building the future as a better and more loving place. This blending of personal narrative and poetic craft creates a space where vulnerability meets artistry, making each poem a window into a life that is both deeply personal and universally human. A poetry memoir doesn't just tell a story, it sings it.

Thank you for sharing your poetry and memoirs about your life, family, and friends. It is an honor to be included with our FAU students in this touching book.

– Dr. Susannah Brown, professor, visual art education,
Florida Atlantic University,
internationally recognized author and artist

In her latest book, *Who am I?*, Vera Ripp Hirschhorn presents us with a mix of prose, poetry and historical context. It's not only a powerful memoir but a self-help for those navigating grief and searching for "authentic self," providing checklists and writing prompts. The book is a love letter to America and conveys her emotional journey as an immigrant along with the devastating and tragic circumstances of her family during WW2. She also explores her deep connections with Spain with moving poetry and anecdotes. This is a unique memoir that will appeal to a broad audience.

> – Angela Page, writer, film producer, and author. President of the South Florida chapter of Women's National Book Association

The cover speaks to the wonders of the poetic journey that lies within. Each part of the collection is a treasure trove of poetic forms, accompanying historical and family photographs, and exercises providing the reader opportunities to dig deeper into the poet's story. Among my favorites are "The Bowl", a situation that could not be solved even with the wisdom of King Solomon and "I Only See a Child" (we have more in common than not). Get ready to partake in some remarkable, memorable memoir moments.

> – Suzanne S. Austin-Hill, Author of *Sixty-seven Pages from the Heart*

Wow, so much to unpack in your story. A-MAZ-ING!...Thank you for sharing it with me.

> – Merrie Meyers, Ph.D., APR, Fellow PRSA

In this engrossing memoir, the author describes the challenges she encountered after arriving here from war-torn Europe in 1952... Later on, the little immigrant who functioned as a working [translator] for her parents became an award-winning student in both high school and college, all of which led to pursue her dream with studies in Spain. Over the years, she put her heart and soul into various forms of teaching.... It is now 2025 and another stage of life. As Hirschhorn conveys in both her prose and poetry, she has begun listening to an inner voice that has turned toward fulfilling her own needs.

– Marlene Klotz, award-winning poet, playwright, and author of nine books

Vera Hirschhorn's life has been interesting yet challenging. Knowing where she has been and what she had to overcome is inspirational. She recounts her evolution through the poetry and prose of her book. Being able to write poems in English is admirable. Yet, being able to translate some of her poems into Spanish is even more admirable. Hirschhorn also shares her practices of breath work and visualizations.

– Alene Model, Teacher of Spanish

Who Am I?

Stepping Stones to Self-Discovery

(Loving Me is Loving You)

a Poetic/Prose Memoir

by
Vera Ripp Hirschhorn, M.S.

© 2025 Vera Ripp Hirschhorn, M.S.
All rights reserved
No part of this book may be used or reproduced in any manner whatsoever without written permission. No part of this book may be stored in a retrieval system or transmitted in any form or by any means including electronic, electrostatic, magnetic tape, mechanical photocopying, recording, or otherwise without the prior permission in writing of the publisher.
Cover Art: Peter Cade, Getty Images
Cover design: Lucy Arnold
Editing and Proofreading: Jessica Temple

Who Am I? Stepping Stones to Self-Discovery
Library of Congress Control Number: 2025921657
ISBN: 978-1-950251-19-3 (paperback)
ISBN: 978-1-950251-20-9 (Ebook)
Hirschhorn, Vera Ripp, 1946 –
First edition
Printed in the United States of America
Published by
National League of American Pen Women, Inc.
PEN WOMEN PRESS

Founded in 1897,
National League of American Pen Women, Inc.
is a nonprofit dedicated to promoting the arts.
1300 17th Street NW, Washington, D.C. 20036-1973
www.nlapw.org

Return to the land of your soul

Return to who you are,
Return to what you are,
Return to where you are
born and reborn again.

-Lyrics by Rabbi Shlomo Carlsbach

Contents

Who Am I? xvii
Preface: Who Am I? xix
Part One: Who I Was (Loving You) 1
Chapter One: Childhood 3
    Introduction: America Welcomed Me! 4
    My Dad's Story 10
    The Bowl 18
    In Springtime I Was Born 20
    En Primavera 21
    Who Are My Songbirds? 22
    Mom, My Role Model 23
    I Was So Proud of You, Dad! 24
    Nose Bleeds 25
    Dad & Civil Rights 26
    Love Letter to Uncle Imre, My Hero of Hashomer Hatzair 27
    My Extraordinary Brother 28
    In Memory of My Beloved Brother 29
    My First Best Friend 30
    Because of You 31
Poems Written in My Adulthood while Reflecting on My Childhood .33
    Life Amidst the Ashes 34
    Perceptions & Realities 35
    The Wall 36
    Breath & Visualization Exercise 38
    Planting Seeds for Your Story 39
Chapter Two: College 41
    Introduction: España Te Quiero 42
    Flamenco's Cultural Roots 50
    It Was You! 52
    An Ode to Sleep 53
    España 54
    My Perfect Past 55
    El Pasado Perfecto 56
    There Was a Time She Felt Alive! 57
    Había una Vez Que Se Sintió Viva 58

And She Smiled 59
Returning to the Land of Sancho and Quijote 61
Breath & Visualization Exercise 62
Planting Seeds for Your Story 63
Chapter Three: Marriage & Children 65
Introduction: Marriage: Serendipity 66
The Child in You 68
Haiku 70
Why Do I Love? 71
I See… 72
Motherhood 73
Blessings In Disguise 75
Remember, Garrin? 76
Remember, Genene? 77
For the Love of Music 79
Happy Father's Day… 81
Your Essence, My Daughter 82
The Love of a Child 83
I'm So Grateful You're My Son 84
I'm So Grateful You're My Daughter 86
What My Kids Have Taught 88
My Greatest Teachers 89
Genene's Letter 90
Garrin's Poem 92
Garrin's Letters 93
Genene's Songs 97
Make Me Happy 98
You in My Dreams 99
Soulmate 101
Love Remains 103
Celebrating Our Love 105
Eulogy for Genene Gila Hirschhorn, 1970-2023 106
Connecting Soul to Soul 108
The Everlasting Light 109
How Do You Turn Grief into Gain? 110
Breath & Visualization Exercise 112
Planting Seeds for Your Story 113

Part Two: Who I Became (Loving Me) 115
Chapter Four: Passions: Arts, Nature, Education 117
Introduction: The Light between Us 119
Arts 123
    My Garden, A Collage 124
    Sounds of Music 125
    Ode To… 126
    The Dance of Life 127
    A Sensory Experience 128
Nature 129
    Nature 130
    Nowhere 131
    Where Have I Gone? 132
    "Vinegar into Honey" 133
    My Rainbow 134
    Drinking from the Poetry of Life 135
    Springtime 136
    La Primavera 137
    The Sands of Time 138
    Nature Speaks…Man Interrupts 139
    The Baby Woodstorks in the Wetlands 140
    Las Cigüeñas Americanas en los Humedales 141
    Fun in the Sun 142
    A Meditation 143
    Una Meditación 144
    Reflections of You 145
    Returning to Me 146
    Nature's Cure 147
    O Strong, Sacred Rock 148
    The Ocean Breathes 149
    My Companions at Sea 150
    I Only See a Child 151
    Hurricane Matthew 152
    Hurricane, 2024 153
    The Dance of the Bonsai 154
    Trees Are People Too! 155
    He Made Eye Contact with Her 156

Clouds 157
Change—It's Inevitable! 158
What the Mountains Teach 159
Haiku 160
Right Here, Right Now 161
Education 163
Education 165
Teaching for Social Change 167
Volunteering 169
Breath & Visualization Exercise 170
Planting Seeds for Your Story 171
Part Three: Who I Am Today (Loving Me Is Loving You) 173
Chapter Five: Passion with Purpose 175
Introduction: Man's Search for Meaning, Discovering Our
Passion with Purpose 176
How Can You Discover Your "Passion with Purpose"? 178
Bullying Awareness 179
Traveling Within 181
Truth Became My Teacher 182
Transformation 183
Transitions 184
"Who Am I?" 186
I Am… 187
I'm Somebody & So Are You! 188
Examples of My Passion with Purpose Projects 189
Spirit of Heroes Competition 190
Excerpts of Students' Award-Winning Stories 191
America's Young Heroes Contests and Programs 192
Song 193
Videos 195
Stories 196
Poetry 197
Educational Resources 201
A Journal for You 203
Teens Are Heroes, Too! 204
I'm Somebody & So Are You! 206
Examples of Official Proclamations and Honors 207

Scholarships 208
Breath & Visualization Exercise 212
Planting Seeds for Your Story 213
Chapter Six: Spiritual Awakenings 215
Introduction 216
There's Light across the Lake 218
In My Solitude 219
Oh, Lights of My Sabbath 221
Nowadays 222
Hoy Dia 223
In Storms 224
Friendships 225
Friendships 226
I Am a Bubble 227
Freedom Now 228
What Is Happiness? 229
On My Road to Me 230
Taking Care of Me 231
Clearly I See 232
I Celebrate… 233
My Harmonious Heart 234
Mi Corazón Armonioso 235
A Path to Paradise 236
Un Camino de Amor 237
What Is Life? 238
"Going Home" 239
Loving Me Is Loving You 240
Breath & Visualization Exercise 242
Planting Seeds for Your Story 243
Acknowledgements 245
About the Author 249
Endnotes 251

Who Am I?

I am the toddler jumping up and down, waving my arms and shouting "Da! Da!" in my playpen upon seeing my dad, on leave from Tito's Army.

I am the little two-year-old leaving her birthplace in a nearly capsized Radnik, en route to the Promised Land.

> I am the child who went forth!

I am the three-year-old dressed in white, walking with other children in rhythm to someone's accordion in front of bombed-out buildings during a holiday.

I am the puffy-faced little refugee staring into a camera in the Promised Land and leaving the warring children of Abraham.

> I am the child who went forth!

I am the six-year-old en route to the Land of the Free on KLM Airlines, clutching a little doll and arriving as a sponsored immigrant along with her younger red-headed brother and parents.

I am the child who was introduced to a new family and taught English by cousins and Mrs. Adler.

> I am the child who went forth!

I am the child who became a citizen with my parents and chose to become one again on my own at sixteen, with tears in my eyes each time I sang "O say can you see...."

I am the child who went forth as the first family member to enroll in college and study in Spain where my soul connected to those of my ancestors;
Where I tasted tapas;
Sang cante hondos and danced to the rhythm of the sevillanas, rhumba, tango, and other flamenco variations.

This was the land where my soul thrived, played, and loved; The fearful ego-driven child transcended, ascended, and expanded into another realm.

Two years after returning home,
The child went forth into the arms of her true
love and became a bride
and soon after, a caretaker, a nurturer who held two shining, sparkling pure gems in her own arms.

The child, in her forties, went forth even in her darkest times, and she found light through her poems, drawings, watercolors, and guitar.

The child today is releasing regrets and resistance to what is and returning to the land of her Soul, loving herself, and sharing the love with others.

I am that child.

PREFACE:
Who Am I?

As you read my story in prose and verse, which has helped me begin to "return home" to my authentic self, I hope it inspires you to begin to tell yours and "return home" to your authentic self as well. Please allow any emotions and/or pain, *if they should arise*, to flow on the waves of acceptance and eventually free you from the past.

For me, one of the most painful experiences I ever felt arose upon the passing of my beloved parents. A wise rabbi offered me the choice to be "distraught or distracted," and I settled with the latter. I began to reflect on their legacy and on my purpose. Reviewing their horrific experiences with genocide due to hatred, prejudice, and religious intolerance, I realized that their "gift" and my purpose were intertwined and linked to teaching tolerance, self-kindness, self-respect, and kindness and respect for others.

Years later, my Pandora's box of deeply held emotions began to erupt like a volcano with its red-hot lava. I never cried in my youth; in fact, I grew up smiling and always cheerful amidst the fearful, angry feelings I felt upon hearing the tragic stories of the senseless murder of my grandparents, aunts, uncles, and four little cousins in Auschwitz[1]. They perished due to one madman's inner rage and desperate need for power and his fearful puppets who were antisemites and just following orders.

Thanks to my son who initiated my therapeutic "back to my

roots" journey to Europe and my daughter's research on my dad's older brother, my Uncle Imre, as well as my husband's accompanying me, I slowly began to face the ego emotions and demons that were tightly suppressed within my subconscious. In his online research, my son located a woman in Chicago whose mother and brother were still living in Galanta, Slovakia, my mom's birthplace. The woman's mother happened to have been in Auschwitz with one of my mom's older sisters.

We decided that our first stop would be Budapest, where my parents met in 1945 upon their liberation from the Ghetto by the Russians[2]. A cute story that I recall hearing in my youth is that my dad wanted to return to his birthplace, Novi Sad, in the former Yugoslavia, (today, Serbia) and asked some of the liberated women if any wanted to accompany him. They all did, and he chose my mom. After many weeks of traveling by horse and buggy, these two malnourished strangers arrived at Dad's empty, ransacked house. Thankfully, the Jewish Community Agency provided them with food, medical treatment, and other necessities. Soon, they had a civil wedding ceremony with one witness.

Upon our first trip to Budapest and our arrival at the airport with its mirrored ceiling, I imagined Hungarian fascists watching us and could literally see them in my mind; I began to sweat, gripped with fear, and felt the need to run. I realized years later that I was reliving Mom's story, told to me in childhood, and her experiences with the Arrow Cross, or Nyilas, during her internment in the Ghetto from 1944-1945. Visiting the four entrances and exits to the Budapest Ghetto reminded me of my mom's courage; she would remove her yellow star and defy the restrictions for Jews in leaving the Ghetto, returning with stolen food that she distributed to the starving, emaciated people within the Ghetto's gates. Upon returning, she always remembered to reattach the yellow star to her coat.

Despite the kindness of the Hungarian guides who led us around the Jewish quarter and the benevolence of tourists, I still felt the inner tension and anxieties. These emotions were heightened upon our departure at the train station en route to Slovakia's capital, Bratislava, and Galanta, especially within our compartment. Upon hearing that conductors were walking around to retrieve our tickets, I began to panic in spite of the two tourists—a cantor and her husband whom we befriended—appearing in our compartment. Once again, I recalled my mom's story—her fleeing from Galanta to Budapest and boarding a train that was swarming with the Arrow Cross. Would you believe I literally felt that the conductors were those same fascists, the Nyilas I knew from hearing my mom's story during my childhood?

My mom, who looked Aryan, had Christian identification papers that her older brother Maurice had purchased and, therefore, was not questioned on the train. Yet, she was forced into the Ghetto as a Jew.

I remember my mom's painful choice, whether to leave her birthplace before the Nazi invasion or stay with her father and older siblings who refused to leave. She begged them to join her to no avail; sadly, they all perished.

Soon after our arrival in Galanta, we met the brother of the American woman from Chicago who drove us to his mom's home. They were absolutely the kindest and sweetest people, who welcomed us with food and drinks. The mother had survived Auschwitz and told me she had met one of my mom's sisters there; sadly, my aunt succumbed to the atrocities. After our lengthy exchange of similar experiences, they drove us to the cemetery, where I was surprised to see a memorial plaque that honored my maternal grandfather, aunts, and uncles. Hours later, the son drove us from Galanta to Bratislava, and on the way, we saw fields and fields of sunflowers aglow in the warm, bright afternoon sun. On our arrival at the capital, we took a train back to Budapest.

It wasn't until years later that I became aware of my parents' survival as being some of the most miraculous, given the inhumane conditions in the Ghetto, such as random shootings, random selections for transport to Auschwitz, starvation, typhoid, and bombings by the Russians. In fact, my mom was sitting next to a young woman who was instantly killed during one of the bombings.

We continued our journey to Novi Sad, Serbia, where my brother and I were born. I was and am grateful to my dearest friend, Fran, who introduced me to someone whose mother-in-law and family lived there during the summer months. It was she who motivated me to return. Her niece welcomed us with open arms and took us to local restaurants and the Holocaust Memorial on the Danube, where all Jews (like my paternal grandfather) and some Serbs were killed during the icy winter of 1942. She also showed me the engraving of my grandfather's name and those of others, in Serbian.

Her kindness showed me a new reality, and not that of my parents' genocidal years. My newfound reality helped me become aware of my truth. In essence, these cathartic trips began my path to liberation from the needless pain, anger, and suffering I held onto for much of my life. Writing "Perceptions and Realities" helped me realize that my childhood fears and anxieties were actually those of my parents' tragic realities, not mine.

Viktor Frankl, author of *Man's Search for Meaning,* was so right in writing that "unnecessary suffering is masochistic rather than heroic." Marshall Stern, author of *Meet the Buddha, Kill the Buddha,* confirmed that "suffering exists," "there is a cause of suffering," and "the cessation of suffering is possible." Clinging to past stories of loss or to future stories of angst perpetuates it. Recalling stories of gratitude for what and who we had and have in our present "now" is another way to release suffering. Knowing that "the only thing in life that's permanent is change" is another. This concept of "impermanence" was and is soothing to some degree in my own personal life.

The book *Many Lives, Many Masters* by psychotherapist Brian Weiss also helped me cope upon the loss of my beloved parents and, more recently, my beloved daughter and brother. This concept of continuous change—whether dealing with the loss of a loved one or in relationships with family, friends, or colleagues, or life's situations at home, school, or work, or with financial status, health, or aging—is our reality. Our challenge is to accept it with a positive attitude.

Grieving and sadness are part of the human condition, as are compassion and non-attachment, Stern stated; suffering is not! As for physical pain, Freud's statement that "unconscious motivations create physical symptoms" has been so true for me. In current times, the work of Dr. John Sarno and Dr. Carl Simonton has shown me that fear and/or anger are the underlying causes of all types of emotional and physical pain and suffering.

What has worked for me, on occasion, is to try to remember that with my free will, I can choose to become more aware of my feelings and acknowledge them, good or bad, with acceptance. In essence, as I wrote in my poem, "Vinegar into Honey," I can choose to feel better and live with gratitude rather than suffer.

I can try to act from my purpose, which is to love myself and others unconditionally for my betterment and the betterment of others, rather than listening to the voice of my ego; that is, fear of physical or ego death, fear of pain or rejection, fear of failure based on past events or imaginings of the future. It's the same voice that keeps us from reaching our potential and fulfilling our dreams and purpose. It's up to us to embrace this voice with acceptance, release it, and move on courageously.

How do I love myself? By taking care of my mind, body, and spirit through healthy nutrition, exercise such as yoga, tai chi, and practicing mindfulness and deep breathing. It's by addressing these needs before addressing the needs of others for the betterment of us all. It's by embracing my story with its strengths and imperfections, which helps me realize that "I'm okay because I'm human." How do I love others? By embracing and listening to their stories with their strengths and imperfections.

I refuse to focus on past mistakes and live with guilt or regret. Rather, I've chosen to learn and grow from my mistakes and thus alleviate suffering further. In a heartwarming book by a palliative nurse[3], she recounted the five regrets expressed by people at the moment of their death:

1. I wish I had the courage to live my life and not the life of others' expectations.
2. I wish I hadn't worked so much.
3. I wish I had the courage to express my feelings.
4. I wish I had been in touch with friends.
5. I wish I had let myself be happier.

Writing WHO AM I? was healing, cathartic, and freeing from the albatrosses of my past. This freedom led me on a journey of self-discovery and self-love.

And so, my dear readers, may my stories in prose and verse, from Childhood through Spiritual Awakenings, inspire you to begin your journey of self-exploration, self-discovery, and self-love, which includes loving your innate perfections, strengths, passions, and unique qualities, as well as your imperfections.

May you be empowered to "return home" to your authentic essence and share and celebrate yourself for your well-being and the well-being of others.

> "I celebrate myself and sing myself
> And what I assume, you shall assume,
> For every atom belonging to me
> As good belongs to you."
>
> -Walt Whitman, *Song of Myself*

PART ONE:
Who I Was
(Loving You)

Chapter One: Childhood

Our first home in the U.S., Maspeth, Queens, New York, 1952.
Photo by cousin Louis Jacobs.

Introduction:
America Welcomed Me!

> *"There was a child went forth every day*
> *And the first object he looked upon and received with wonder, pity, love,*
> *or dread, that object he became,*
> *And that object became part of him for the day,*
> *Or a certain part of the day, or for many years, or*
> *stretching cycles of years."*
> -Walt Whitman

KLM AIRLINES LANDED in New York, January 1952, with my family aboard, thanks to four family sponsors. I, Veritza, age six, disembarked the plane, clutching my little dolly. With me were my five-year-old, freckled, red-headed brother, Hinko (later called Hank), and our parents, survivors of genocide. I was a "miracle" child born in 1946, out of the ashes of war-torn Europe.

America welcomed Dezider and Yelena (later known as Daniel and Judith)—young, resilient, hopeful Holocaust survivors of the ravages of persecution. Their pain would be masked and buried behind forced smiles forever. At least they were alive! Had it not been for Raul Wallenberg who saved the Budapest Ghetto from being bombed by the Nazis, little Veritza and little Hinko would not be here today.

Gone was Yugoslavia's bloodstained Danube[4], her embattled communist birthplace, Novi Sad, and that of her murdered grandparents, aunts, uncles, and little cousins. Gone was death and loss due to crazed power and hate-driven evil madmen and madwomen.

Also left behind was the newly created "Promised Land"[5] in which Veritiza's family arrived in 1948 on the *Radnik*. Absent was their "shack" near the Lebanese border. Out of sight were the milk and bread lines, baby goats, and chicks that nourished their empty bellies. Only a blurred vision of the quarreling, battling children of Abraham remained.

Daddy, how it pained me to feel your anguish and hear your screaming nightmares, jolting me out of a deep sleep every night. How it distressed me to see you disrespected because of your broken English and third-grade education. God knows you did your best to raise a family, living next door to your uncle's steel factory in Maspeth, Queens, where you slaved day and night. Yet, I loved walking there during your night shifts and spending the only quiet and peaceful time I could with you alone.

I was so proud of you as they promoted you to night superintendent. You were always there helping the workers and giving them first aid whenever anyone got hurt on the job.

Mommy, how it saddened me that you earned money as a domestic, cleaning the homes of relatives and strangers alike; and you never complained. You were so happy to bring home second-hand toys, dolls, and clothes. I was so proud to see you learn English and eventually become a certified manicurist.

Rarely did you speak of, nor did I see you cry for, the loss of your father and nine siblings, except the times I heard you in the dark boiler room of our basement. I wish I had asked more questions about your family, including your brother Maurice and his two beautiful children: Eva, age six, and Erin, age eight. Their light was extinguished so very early!

Some of these childhood memories have endured within my spirit like black and white photographs, and memories of my parents' pain and pleasure fueled my feelings for expression. Thankfully, they evoked my poems and eventually, upon their passing, my life's purpose as an educator: to promote self-respect and self-kindness, as well as respect and kindness for each other's diversities, and to prevent bullying, the foundation for genocide.

Early on, I was given the responsibility of translating and interpreting for my parents whether at home, writing the checks, in the offices of physicians, or at stores. Inadvertently, I became a caretaker and parent to my parents, feeling their pain, subconsciously, at having lost twenty-two family members during the Holocaust. "Parenting" them came naturally, and I was a willing daughter—washing dishes, making everyone's beds, ironing, whatever it took to help make their lives easier—without being asked or told to do any of these chores.

In Maspeth, having no neighbors except a pub and my uncle's steel factory, I cherished visits from my American-born cousins Robert, Norman, Artie, Violet, and Mary, with whom I'd always laugh.

I also treasured my younger cousin Mira, and her parents—my Aunt Beba and Uncle Mike—all born in Novi Sad. Other times, in my solitude, I used to pretend I was a teacher taking "roll call" as I checked off the names of my "students."

Who would have thought that my role-playing would become my reality, twenty years later?

I learned English quickly, and classmates soon began inviting me to parties.

As a preteen, I had to take accordion lessons, which, surprisingly, given the fact that I hated the instrument and especially performing in front of family members, led to my passion for music. I would rather have had professional dance classes. I loved to dance and had to settle for dancing and singing with the Dick Clark *Bandstand* dancers on T.V. and D.J. Alan Freed's records on the radio. My love for music is described in the poem, "Mom, My Role Model" in Chapter I and in Chapter IV, Passions.

Later, I shared a friendship heart with Susan Feinstein, one of the popular girls from the "in crowd." Imagine that!

I was becoming Americanized! In fact, in 1957, we became legal citizens; kids automatically became naturalized with their parents. Yet, for some reason, I chose to become a citizen on my own in 1962, at age sixteen.

Also that year, as a sophomore at Flushing High School, my friends and I used to hang out at a candy store at Union Turnpike, Queens. One day while laughing and dancing there, a cop approached me and quietly handed me a piece of paper that I was asked to deliver to my parents. I guess I was having such a good time that I ignored it and just placed it in my pocket.

Upon returning home after my long trek from Union Turnpike, I read the letter to my mom and nearly flipped out.

"How could he give me a summons for wearing short shorts? How could he demand that I appear in court before a judge?" I asked angrily. Suddenly, I, a law-abiding teen, felt like a criminal.

I seemed to be more upset than my parents. I guess I perceived that I let them down. I realize now that I always tried to please them and make them happy since I felt that they had suffered enough during their wartime atrocities.

The next day, I told my neighbor, Margie, about it, and she had a brilliant idea: "Get a pair of shorts that are shorter than what you wore and talk your way out of it with the comparison," she advised.

The day I was to appear in court finally arrived, and I felt so ashamed and embarrassed that my dad had to lose a workday to take me to the Queens Courthouse on the subway. Once inside, the judge called me to the bench and asked me to tell my version of the story. "Your Honor, I'd like to contest the summons." He smiled and asked me to continue. And so, I demonstrated that the shorts I wore were longer than the ones I held up for comparison; this contrast seemed to convince the judge. Imagine my joy when he said the charges were dismissed!

That was one of the most difficult experiences in my teen years, and I was so grateful to my neighbor and my dad and mom and, of course, the judge.

During the hot, humid months, we shared a bungalow with Aunt Irene and cousins Louie and Francis on Beach 17, Far Rockaway, Queens. Dad visited us on the weekends. My endless love for the ocean stems from those tranquil summers. I've written several poems dedicated to my muse, the ocean, which I've included in Chapter IV, Passions.

"I am that child that went forth"
-Walt Whitman

What's your story?
Be that child that went forth!
(Let objects, people, places, and memories become part of that child who went forth every day.)

Vera, age three, Israel, 1949.

My Dad's Story

As told to Garrin Evan Hirschhorn, his grandson, 1991

I WAS BORN in Novi Sad, Yugoslavia, on July 24, 1922, to Hinko and Marie Rip, and named Dezider. At a young age, I was educated to be an upholsterer and carpenter. I had my own shop in our home in Novi Sad until 1941. In April, the Nazis occupied my birthplace, and I had to do forced labor such as cleaning streets and construction.

Upon my return, my parents felt I should leave for Budapest, Hungary, and stay with cousins, since more and more young Jewish boys were being taken away to working camps. So I lived with relatives and soon got a job and my own apartment. Sometime afterward, my mom also left Novi Sad for her protection and went to Baya, Hungary, to stay with her cousins.

My dad remained in Novi Sad. One day, my landlady—whose son was an officer in the military and stationed in Novi Sad—informed me that my father was among those killed during the slaughter from January 21-23, 1942, by the Hungarian collaborators. They removed their belongings, including rings and watches, and told them to lie down in the snow-covered, frigid streets, and then murdered them. My dad, the elderly, women, and children—whether dead or alive—were all thrown into the icy, frozen, bloody waters of the Danube River.[1]

I went to Baya to be with my mom and didn't tell her of my father's death, so as not to worry her. We just told her that he was missing. She left Baya and traveled night and day looking for my dad and eventually learned of his death. Soon after, we were told that it was safe to return to Novi Sad, where I continued to work in my trade for a few months, during which time I earned enough money to provide my mom with food and other necessities. I tried to calm her during these hard times.

From 1942-1944, I was forced out of my home by the Hungarians and Germans to working camps in different locations. First, I was taken to Kovačica, near Novi Sad, to work the mines and build military bunkers and offices for the Nazis. Then, I was transported with other Jewish males in a cattle train—without food for one week—to a labor camp at the Hungarian border near Galicia. Here, we were commanded to cut down trees and build wooden roads and bridges. We were then transferred to Tatahago, on a high hill, to work the mines so that the Hungarians and Germans could prevent the Russians from invading.

While a prisoner in slave labor camps, I was wounded in the leg during crossfire between Germans/Hungarians and the Russians and taken to a military hospital where the doctor insisted on amputating my leg because of gangrene. The doctor's assistant, who happened to be a "righteous" Croatian from Yugoslavia, pleaded with the doctor to save my leg; in fact, he promised the doctor that he would take special care of it. My leg was in a cast from my toes to my knee for three months. I received crutches from a Hungarian military doctor, and a kind Hungarian priest offered to help me as well.

Soon after, I had to return to the camps where the Hungarian soldiers began beating us—our heads, our shoulders, and our entire bodies—with belts and threatened to kill us because we were Jews. They began to starve us and work us hard. Some of us had to pull a horse and buggy with heavy ammunition and build military offices and roads.

We had to sleep in the woods under all weather conditions; our clothes and shoes began to disintegrate to the point that the shoes no longer had soles on them. We were always hungry. We managed to find dirty potatoes and drank green, polluted rainwater. Many men developed dysentery. I ran a fever for days and was skin and bones and was so weak that I would fall each time I tried to stand up. But I never gave up hope of seeing my mother once again. God gave me strength.

The Hungarian military only fed us green lettuce cooked in water that was filled with so much sand that our teeth hurt while eating it. We drank muddy, filthy dishwater, which the Hungarians said was coffee. We never saw bread or meat.

We had to continue to put mines in the roads, deeper and deeper. We began to freeze, and I remembered my dad's survival stories when he served in WWI. So, I began to constantly rub my face, hands, feet, and all body parts to keep the blood circulating and prevent frostbite. I taught the others to do the same, and we managed to survive. Sometimes, the Hungarians would begin shooting at random and kill some of the men. Once, I whispered to the survivors to lie down and pretend they were dead if and when the shooting began again.

In 1944, the Hungarian military wanted to remove weak, wounded Jews like me from Hungary and ship us to Germany, but the German soldiers would only permit strong, healthy Jews to go to Germany. One hundred thirteen survived the slave labor camps, including me. We were then sent to the Budapest Ghetto, where seventy thousand Jews were imprisoned and where I met my wife, your grandmother, Yelena, who was born in Galanta, Czechoslovakia.

Yelena used to remove the yellow Star of David that we all had to wear and sneak out of the Ghetto with her falsified Christian identification papers that her older brother Moric gave her. Under the pretense of friendship with a local Nazi soldier, she accepted his invitations to dinner. While he paid for the meal, Yelena would steal bread and quickly place any remaining food into her big black coat's inside pockets. Returning to the Ghetto, she distributed the food to the starving, cold, emaciated, disease- and lice-infested Jewish prisoners. Her other brother, Josef, buried many of the dead. Repeated violent assaults were carried out in the Ghetto, often by members of the Arrow Cross, many of whom were about fifteen years of age.

Heavy bombing by the Russians, which killed your grandmother's friend, was most severe when the Russians surrounded Budapest in late December 1944. We learned later that the SS soldiers of the Reich and Arrow Cross had planned a pogrom in the Ghetto with firing squads. The planned massacre was canceled thanks to Raoul Wallenberg, who threatened the German SS general that if he didn't stop it, he would personally see to it that the general would be charged with murder and genocide by the War Crimes Tribunal. Days later, the Russians entered and liberated the Ghetto.

Upon liberation by the Russians on January 17 and 18, 1945, I invited Yelena and a man to return to Novi Sad, Yugoslavia, with me. We traveled three to four weeks by horse and buggy. We stopped at farms to sleep but couldn't eat anything because of our stomach problems. Upon arriving in Novi Sad to my family's empty home, your grandmother and I got married in the State House and ate food provided by the United Jewish Appeal.

Soon, I was told that my mom, Marie Berger Rip; my sister, Irene; and her two little children, Elvira, age eleven, and Mira, age seven, were rounded up—along with nineteen hundred other Jews—in the Novi Sad Synagogue for two weeks and then transported to Auschwitz, where they were gassed in 1944. As for one of my older brothers, Imre, I was told that he was drafted into the Yugoslav Army and had to go to Germany but escaped[6].

Elvira, eleven, and Mira, seven, killed at Auschwitz. Compliments of the Ripp family.

Your grandmother learned that her widowed father and seven of her nine siblings, as well as her niece, Eva, age six, and nephew, Ervin, age eight, all perished in the genocide known later as the Holocaust.

Eva Friebert, six, and Ervin Friebert, eight. Compliments of the Friebert family.

We decided to have children, and our baby Vera was born in 1946; she was named after her maternal grandmother, Veronica. A year later, Hank was born and named after my father, Hinko. Soon I was drafted into Tito's Army and spent six months near Novi Sad and six months in Sarajevo. It was tough under Tito's social communism. There was no freedom; there was strict law and order. Both parents had to work for the government. Yelena refused, so she was constantly harassed and always made up excuses that she was sick, had headaches, and so on. She never allowed our children to stay in the government daycare centers.

We were all harassed by the authorities. At random, they would stop us in the streets or knock at our door and ask about our purchases. Everything was bought with government stamps—even our food. Each family had allocations. Our family had a vegetable garden, and we raised chickens and geese. We also had clothing limitations. In 1948, Tito permitted Jewish survivors to emigrate to Israel.

After surviving the *Radnik*'s near capsize, my family arrived in Haifa soon after it received statehood. We were greeted by some Israelis who took us to Kiryat Yam, near Haifa. Soon after our arrival, I was drafted but was so mentally, emotionally, and physically exhausted, that I received an exemption.

Life was very hard where we lived in a shack near the Lebanese border in Bassa or Betzet in the Western Galilee in northern Israel, near Nahariya. We had bread and milk lines and constant attacks. The war between the Arabs and Israelis escalated so much that we had to live with my brother and his family for eight months in Haifa. Upon our return, the government gave us a small farm with chickens and goats, which provided us with eggs and milk.

In 1952, we left for America on board KLM Airlines, thanks

to the sponsorship of my mother's two brothers, and my older brother, who provided us with employment and housing next to the steel factory where I worked.

Questions to Think About

1. Is my dad's story of prejudice, bigotry, and hatred in Europe from 1938-1945 relevant today in our society, across the country and the world? If so, how? Consider the rise in hate crimes.
2. Why do you think people hate or have prejudice? Is it their upbringing? Is it intentional ignorance about people of a different race, religion, ethnicity, or sexuality?
    a. Is it due to a lack of willingness or knowledge and their feelings of insignificance? Or do they hate due to fear of change and losing control?
    b. How can you, as an individual or with others such as classmates, friends, or family, help lessen different types of hate?
3. Have you or someone you know ever been shamed, humiliated, bullied, or discriminated against? If so, how did it feel? How did you or the other person respond? Did anyone witness it? If so, did they help or just stand by and observe it?
4. Have you ever felt fear of physical pain or death? Or fear of rejection, criticism, or even fear of failure? If so, how did you deal with any one of those fears? Did you choose to accept it or resist it?
5. Why do you think bullies act out violently towards others and even themselves? Consider the rise in school shootings and the rise in teen suicide.

6. Did you know that the intent of the genocide of the Jewish people in Nazi Europe was to completely exterminate them because of their religion? Are you aware that half of Jewish children—over one million—were killed because of their faith and being too young to work? How could you honor them and give them a voice?
7. Would you be inspired to research and read the stories of these children or the testimonies of the hidden children on the website of Yad Vashem in Israel or the U.S. Raoul Wallenberg Holocaust Museum in Washington, D.C.? If so, how could their personal stories be implemented in lesson plans? Have you considered organizing an interview in your classroom or community with living hidden children? How could they help students?
8. If you had lived during the European genocide of the 1930s and 1940s, in what ways do you feel you would have responded? Would you have joined the resistance fighters? Would you have participated in rescue missions?
9. What other genocides are you familiar with? Do you feel that "atrocities belong to all of us and that we are responsible for the possibilities that allowed for the perpetrators, collaborators, and bystanders to actively participate or look away"?
10. In your opinion, what are the lessons of the genocides of the 20th century? How can they be taught? How can we focus on humanity's weaknesses as well as humanity's strength and human-ness? Are there any signs that history could repeat itself nowadays?

The Bowl

Upon my return to Israel in 1994 as an adult, my husband, Marty, and I landed in a country where many cities were actively being bombed. These events did not stop me from seeking a guide to drive us to Betzet, the village near the Lebanese border where I spent ages two to six.

After passing through areas bombed out in the late 1940s, our guide, Avi, finally stopped in Betzet, and I saw a woman about my age in the street. I tried to converse in English, then in Spanish, then in French, and even in Hungarian...but to no avail. She didn't respond. My last recourse was our guide, whom I had asked to inquire, in Hebrew, if she had ever heard of the Ripp family.

To our surprise, she had. "Oh, my God," I screamed, "that's my family! We lived here from 1948 to 1952." She, after introducing herself as Robin, graciously motioned to invite us into her home and set the table with fruit, cheese, wine, and other goodies. As soon as Marty, Avi, and I sat down, our cordial hostess politely got up and returned with a large, colorful, floral bowl.

"This bowl," she said, "belonged to your mom, and my mom bought it from yours just before your family left for America. Your family needed all the money they could get and sold most of the few possessions they had."

I asked our guide to ask her if I could buy it, and she said, "Oh, no, this means so much to me since it was my mom's."

I said I would pay anything to have it as it was also my mom's.

"Sorry," she replied in Hebrew, "no money could replace my feelings for this bowl."

What else could I have said or done? As we left and thanked her for her hospitality, we hugged and exchanged phone numbers and addresses. "Yes, I understand," I said, as tears rolled down my face.

Family collage with photo of Vera as an infant, center. Collage by Vera Hirschhorn.

In Springtime I Was Born

Ekphrastic poem Inspired by Ruth Weiss'
Spring Path at Jupiter Ridge

For You,
Springtime created joy.
In Springtime, I was born!

For You,
Nature's Divine light
Brought forth a rebirth,
Amidst nightmares of the night.

Wildflowers carved a path of renewal;
And the thorns of the past,
Transformed into Springtime
Of Hope ever-last-ing.

En Primavera

Poema a mis Padres

Para ti,
En primavera, yo nací,
Para ti,
Mucha alegría, ¿verdad que sí?

En primavera,
El renacimiento comenzó,
De nueva familia,
Que en el invierno falleció.

Para ti,
Entre cenizas del pasado
Los girasoles crecieron,
Miraban hacia la luz
En el verano.

En primavera,
El renacimiento empezó
Para mí y
¡Para ti!

Who Are My Songbirds?

Those who *resisted* in small ways;
Those who hid the forbidden;
He who taught others to pretend to be dead,
With his blood-stained wounds.
She, who stole food to give to the emaciated.
And even those who accepted death with Dignity!

Mom, My Role Model

Mom, you asked for so little and gave so much!
Happy with just family: Dad, Hank, and me; And later Marty,
Moe, Nene, Gar, Nikki, Dar, and Dee.

You gave your heart and your voice with song;
Cheering us whenever things went wrong.
While you insisted I have those accordion lessons that
I dreaded and feared,
My passion for music grew year after year.

Giving charity and support for others,
We all learned from you:
And so, your grandkids gave toys to hospitals
and performed at nursing homes for fathers and mothers.

Your love for nature;
The fragrant lilies in our backyard.
Your floral arrangements in baskets adorned with
butterflies and ribbons;
Your bird cages decorated with tiny ceramic bluebirds;
Your porcelain miniature tchotchkes of baby deer,
rabbits, and parrots.

Your playfulness and love for children:
Creating porcelain dolls, painting and dressing them
And building and decorating dollhouses.

Your calmness amidst the chaos during your
sleeping hours, awakening
abruptly to Dad's nightmares.

Your being there before and after school.
Your just being!
Your resilience despite so much pain,
Look how much we've gained!

I Was So Proud of You, Dad!

It's the week of your birth, July 24th
You would have been 98 years old!
You were a caring hot-blooded spirit, with so much grit,
always going here, there, everywhere.

I remember visiting you in your office,
at the steel factory where you worked as the night foreman.
Just me and you alone,
during those rare, peaceful times.

I was so proud of you!

I recall how you removed splinters from my bare feet
at Far Rockaway's boardwalks
and even carrying me out of the cold ocean;
time seemed to stop still.

I was so proud of you!

And I'll always treasure the photo
of you with a cigarette,
dangling from your smiling mouth
that I shared with my friends as a teen.

I was so proud of you!

Nose Bleeds

It was always a mystery;
my history of red fluid dripping from my nose;
and Dad's gooey Vaseline cotton balls,
that cured those recurrent woes.

Dad & Civil Rights

Dad, to me, you began the civil rights
movement in 1960s Miami;
One brave soul at a time:
Drinking from the "colored" water fountains
Defying the status quo with all its crimes!

Giving first aid to workers in the steel factory,
Regardless of race, creed, or ethnicity;
Those images were etched forever in my adolescent mind!
And paved my way to teach self-respect and
respect for diversity.

Given our family's tragic losses in the 1940s,
We know too well its many causes:
Indifference, Hatred, Bigotry!
Repairing my world remains my
Legacy!

Love Letter to Uncle Imre, My Hero of Hashomer Hatzair[7]

Uncle Imre, how I wish I could have met you.

Dad always said that I reminded him of you;
My head, in books day and night.
Dad recalled how fascist thugs beat him up
in place of you since you both looked alike.

Uncle Imre, I felt your strength,
your daringness,
your resistance:
burning, bombing fascist strongholds
to guard, to aid, to save
Our People!

What a Blessing you'll always be in our Family!

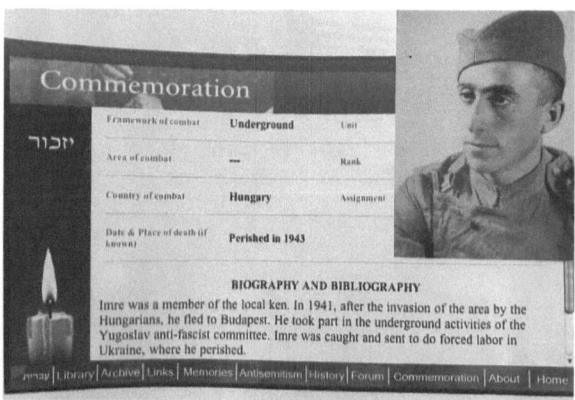

Uncle Imre, my hero, born December 21, 1919,
died during the Shoah in 1943.
Compliments of the Ripp family.

My Extraordinary Brother

Waking me up to your "lights, camera, action,"
You smiling, me shouting, "Are you getting satisfaction?"

Jumping and jiving to 45s/LPs, we rolled and we rocked;
Me in short shorts; you in orange shirt and matching socks.

You doing pushups, sit-ups, or pumping iron,
Juggling basketballs or riding your bike,
You were as strong as a lion!

Watching you strum your Spanish guitar
and I, dancing flamenco
while twirling my shawl around you;
You and me. What a show!

High-energy teens,
With "ordinary" means.

An extraordinary brother,
Unlike any other.

In Memory of My Beloved Brother[8]

HAIKU

My brother has passed;
Cardinals honor his life,
Willows weep, I cry.

Swimming in the sun,
Inspires, energizes;
Uplifts my sad mood.

The ocean glistens;
Water surrounds all around.
It soothes. I'm at peace.

My First Best Friend

What a surprise!
Who would have surmised?
That my very first poem
Would be remembered and prized;
By my very first friend
Who verbalized, 57 years later:

"All around me things are blue
Listen and I'll name a few.
The sky, the sea, the murmuring brook
The cover of my English book;
My boyfriend's eyes so warm and sweet;
The brand new Ford just down the street."

I hugged her as we socialized,
So grateful for her gift;
And most of all for my first friendship
With a beautiful girl from Flushing Township.

Because of You

for Mrs. Adler, my 5th grade English teacher

Because of You,
a six-year-old immigrant girl
from lands of hate,
felt joy in the Land of the Free.

Because of You,
I learned to speak,
to write, to hear
in the language of freedom.

Because of You,
children loved me more;
boys pulled my hair;
girls became my friends.

Because of You,
I became Mom's helper;
Dad's protector;
My brother's tutor.

Because of You,
I excelled in school.

Because of You
I wanted to teach.

Poems Written in My Adulthood while Reflecting on My Childhood

Life Amidst the Ashes

dedicated to my dad's liberation

Yes, I was life amidst the ashes;
Liberation at last!
Gone were your lashes
Gone were the blasts!

Fear reigned
Your nightmares pained
Adrenaline flowed
Seeds were sowed.

I lived your war
Far too long.
We're free my beloveds;
Hear our eternal song:

Victims, no more.
Victims, no more.
At long last,

Victims no more!

Perceptions & Realities

Our childhood Perceptions are an illusion of our Truth.

My "back to roots" journey to Budapest,
Galanta, and Novi Sad,
Awoke me to my newfound reality;
To the Oneness of "Now."

My journey began to stir up the slumber of youthful
"realities" from the past

Though their nightmares never passed:

Slave labor camps, malnourishment; muddy dishwater for coffee; dirty, earth-laden potatoes and "soup" of green, polluted rainwater; sandy, cooked green lettuce for food; beatings with belts; disintegrated clothes and shoes; dysentery, fever.

Dad's reality
Not mine!

Emaciated, starving, bone-weary living corpses; abandoned dead corpses buried by Jews like my uncle Josef. Lice, shaven heads; yellow stars sewn on coats; swastikas, rifles, shootings; Hungarian/German Nazis swarming inside, outside, and around the Budapest Ghetto, the halfway house to death.

Mom's reality
Not mine!

My "now" felt their courage, their strength, their resilience.
My "back into the future" inhaled and exhaled the breath
of relief and renewal.

The Wall

in the Budapest Ghetto

In memory of my parents,
heroic survivors,
Daniel and Judith Friebert Rip

Only remnants remain of hate and fear,
Only a reminder of yesteryear.
Who created the wall?
Are they still here?
Never again! Never again!
Let it be known.
Never again!

The wall divides, nothing grows!
A bridge unites over water that flows!
Water heals.
Life begins.
Never again! Never again!
Let it be known.
Never again!

Look over there!
Flowers in bloom:
Pink ones, red ones, purples and gold.
Gone is the wall.
Gone is the doom.
Will hate and fear ever resume?
Never again! Never again!
Let it be known,
Never again!

Actual wall remnant of the Budapest Ghetto that separated the prisoners within and the outside world. Photo by Vera Hirschhorn.

The plaque on the wall is in Hungarian and translates:

Remembered

In Eternal Remembrance of the Day, Forty Years Ago When the Soviet Army, Liberating Our Country, Destroyed the Walls Surrounding the Only Remaining European Ghetto.

1945 January 18-1985 January 18

The wall has since been destroyed.

Breath & Visualization Exercise

Imagine yourself at sunrise.
As you feel the warming of the sun,

Breathe out tension through your mouth.
Breathe in relaxation through your nose.

Slowly breathe out negativity.
Slowly breathe in positivity.

Slowly breathe out the past
And breathe in the present, pleasant moment.

Now imagine the sun's light shining on the top of your head.

Feel it flow down to your eyes,
relaxing them with healthy sight and insights.

Feel it soothe your throat and your heart
with feelings of love, empathy, and compassion.

Feel it flow down to your belly, calming and
empowering it gently.
Feel the light relax your sacrum. And lastly, your tailbone.

Soon, your inner voice asks you: *What blessings have I received today, yesterday and this past week? From whom?*

As the balmy breezes begin to bring you back
to the present moment,
You feel more refreshed, revitalized, and ready to
start a brand-new day.

Planting Seeds for Your Story

Getting to Know You, Your Feelings, Your Emotions, Your Thoughts

1. Select one poem that resonates or connects with your heart and soul.
2. Ask yourself:

    - Why did I select this poem?
    - What does it remind me of? What happened? What feelings arose?
    - Who was involved?
    - Where did this occur?
    - When did it happen?

3. Express your story in any format by writing a poem, essay, play, novel, or lyrics to a song, sketching, drawing, photographing, or making a video.

    - Who were you in the past?
    - Who did you become?
    - Who are you today?
    - Did anyone or anything have an impact or influence on you that might have contributed to who you were, became, or are today?
    - How can you use your story for social change?

4. Did you discover any new revelations from telling your story? Did it resolve any issues? Did you share it with another?
5. How did you feel upon completing your story? Write for three pages, without stopping, without any concern for spelling or grammar.

Chapter Two: College

Vera, Madrid, 1966, enroute to Granada, Spain.
Photo by a classmate.

Introduction:
España Te Quiero

Who could have imagined that an immigrant young girl from Queens College would live like a "Queen" for a year?

THANKS TO A dear friend who asked what my plans were after high school, I applied to Queens College. I don't recall ever discussing any higher education goals with my immigrant parents; after all, my dad was a carpenter in his teens and mom a manicurist before the years of atrocities ruined their opportunities for more education in their native countries. Here, in their new land of opportunities, they were too overwhelmed with making a living, dad working nights in a steel factory and mom a domestic and eventually a manicurist to make ends meet.

Admission to Queens College was very competitive, yet affordable for students like me. My "hard work and some play" in high school paid off. What a liberal arts education I received just for $24 and textbooks per semester!

How fortunate for me that my family eventually moved to Flushing, New York, where Queens College was within walking distance. Its library became my home away from home, day and night, night and day. It was my sanctuary where peace and calm reigned.

And who knew that Walt Whitman's tie to Queens College with its original Spanish-style buildings were premonitions of some of my passions today: poetry, especially *Leaves of Grass,* and the Spanish language and culture?

A boulder just outside the Student Union building marks the

original location of the one room schoolhouse where Walt Whitman taught.

Thanks to Queens College, unforeseen doors opened from 1964-1968 that contributed to creating the woman I am today. They included my junior year in Granada, Spain, as an exchange student in the college's study abroad program. Even today, I consider those years to be some of the happiest highlights in my life.

Who would have thought that I'd be honored at the University of Granada as "Miss Foreigner" and serenaded by the "Tuna," a group of students in traditional university dress who played traditional instruments such as the bandurria, lute, guitar, and tambourine?

Funny how I began as a foreigner in Israel and then was again a foreigner in America and again in Spain.

I was totally immersed in the Spanish language and culture, living, eating, and sleeping in Doña Eugenia's home with two other students, one roommate from Queens College and another from Leeds, England, who was studying the Arabic language and culture. Taking showers was challenging as we waited about 20 minutes for the hot water. I became a bit homesick during the cold winter months as I longed for the cozy warmth back in the States. Here, we were only provided with a small heater under the dinner table to warm our legs.

A typical day included lunch at 2:30, followed by a siesta and late dinner, with lots of olive oil. Yummy snacks included chocolate on bread. Occasionally, we would go to the tapas bars and indulge in mussels, garlic shrimp, monkfish, or cod.

Walking around Granada was an experience not only because of the need to replace my custom-made shoes every few months due to the cobblestones but also because of the *piropos* or "compliments" by the males of the city. Shouting, "*Guapetona!*" or "Beautiful!" at all the young females was in good nature and not with mal intent.

As for classes, I attended the University of Granada, specifically, the College of Philosophy and Letters. We studied medieval art, architecture, literature, and history alongside the Spanish university students, with whom I studied for exams in the center of town at Café Granada. One of my greatest pleasures was reading Cervantes' *Don Quijote* in the original Spanish and the plays and poetry of Federico García Lorca. To this day, I adore the work of both writers.

Imagine studying in the gardens of the Generalife with its fountains, roses, grapevines, and Arabic tiles, surrounded by the beauty of Granadino palaces like the Alhambra and the Sierra Nevada mountains! I felt as if I were in Paradise!

Imagine listening to Gypsies sing their soulful flamenco* cantes accompanied by strumming guitarists in the neighborhood of Sacromonte, where they lived in whitewashed caves cut into rock. Imagine learning to dance flamenco with a young, spirited, enthusiastic, talented, and beautiful gitana (Gypsy). How happy and grateful I was to experience the magical, authentic flavor of the flamenco dance as she repeated the heel, toe steps—"ta ca ton, ta ca ton; taca, taca, taca ton,"—in her black, high-heeled, custom-made flamenco shoes. I was one of the fortunate students to do so in my spare time. Other students learned to play the flamenco guitar.

Among the many joys of studying in Granada were the side trips we took with our American Resident Director and his wife. On long weekends, we travelled to many places such as Palma de Mallorca, Caen, Gibraltar, Toledo, and Andalucian cities like

Sevilla, Málaga, and Córdoba. In these cities, we witnessed the melding of Jewish, Christian, and Arabic cultures reflected in the architecture of synagogues, churches, and mosques. To think that I walked the ancient streets and sites where three religions shared each other's customs, languages, and histories for seven centuries!

During long holidays, I travelled alone over twelve hours by train from Granada to Antwerp, Belgium. It was such a joy to be greeted by my beloved mother's brother, my Uncle Maurice, at the train station. I recognized him immediately from Mom's photos. Arriving to his home, I met my cousin, Vera, for the very first time. We bonded instantly.

We both had so much in common; we were both named Vera in memory of our maternal grandmother, Veronica. Vera was a polyglot who spoke Flemish and Slovakian in addition to the French, Hungarian, and English we both spoke. We both loved French music, and to this day, I have her record albums of Enrico Macias, a famous Moroccan singer of the 1960s. What enchanting music! What a gift she gave me! Upon my departure, we agreed to write to each other. For decades we sent letters and cards to each other; she in French and I in English to practice each other's languages. I also sent her miniature perfume bottles to add to her collection.

Vera's stepmother was certainly no replacement for her beloved mother, though she was very kind and complimentary to me; in fact, she bought me a green winter overcoat, a black handbag, and a purple sweater which I still wear in cold temperatures today. I only wish she would have been as kind to my precious cousin Vera. Uncle Maurice, she, and Vera surprised me one evening and took me to a popular Hungarian restaurant where the Gypsies played on the violin familiar tunes which my parents had sung to me in my childhood. The performers danced the czardas, a well-known folk dance. I'm so glad that I had the opportunity to meet my dear Mom's family; sadly, my mom and her brother never saw each other again until she flew to Europe for his funeral.

Vera was such a beautiful soul, and it was sad that she had to live with the ghosts of her brother and sister, both of whom were murdered by the Nazis during World War II. She also endured the pain of the early loss of her mother. We corresponded until her own tragic early passing.

I remember in my childhood that Uncle Maurice sent my mom a gold bracelet and a necklace for me from Tangiers, Morocco, which is where they lived at the time. My younger brother received a gold cup for his Bar Mitzvah; these gifts were brought to us by a family member during her trip to the States.

As a naïve college exchange student, I was never aware of the politics in 1966-67. What I do remember is how our Queens College Director, Robert Smith, instructed all of us to forgo any political discussions within our own group as well as with our Spanish peers at the University of Granada; this included our Spanish families with whom we lived during the year abroad.

To be honest, I wasn't interested in politics and never even knew much of Francisco Franco, the dictator who staged a military coup against the new and legally elected Second Republic of 1931, and who began the Spanish Civil War in 1936. Franco, with the support of Portugal, Fascist Italy, Nazi Germany, and the church, eventually won the war and reigned until 1975. Later on, back in America, I began to understand why we had never been informed that the home of one of my favorite Spanish poets and playwrights, Federico García Lorca, was located in the province of Granada and forbidden to be seen by the general public. Franco ordered his murder in 1936 for being a homosexual. Nowadays, his home is a main attraction for tourists in the area.

After many years, I had also learned of The International Brigades who trekked across the Pyrenees to Spain in 1936 to fight for the legitimacy of the Second Republic and against fascism. They consisted of at least thirty-five thousand volunteers from more than fifty nations, including America's Abraham Lincoln Brigade, organized by communists, in addition to France, Poland, Cuba, Peru, Yugoslavia, and Mexico. These volunteers defied the twenty-seven countries, including the U.S., that chose a non-intervention policy with regard to the Spanish Civil War.

The Brigades existed for two years, from 1936-1938, when all international volunteers were withdrawn by the Spanish Republic from its forces. The International Brigades were strongly supported by the Comintern and represented the Soviet Union's commitment to assisting the Spanish Republic—with arms, logistics, military advisers, and the NKVD (Soviet secret police).

Each brigade was named after a hero. The Naftali Botwin Brigade, for example, was named in honor of their Polish labor activist leader, executed in 1925 for the murder of a police informant. The Brigade comprised mainly of five thousand Jewish volunteers from East European countries, especially Poland. They, with their communist and socialist ideals, came to defend the liberal Spanish republicans against Franco's fascism because this was, in their minds, one way of fighting back Nazism in their own respective countries.

Once back home in Flushing and in need of some money to complete my senior year at Queens College, I decided to tutor Spanish and eventually taught flamenco dance for interested adult education students.

I registered for the necessary education courses that included student teaching. My internship in a Brooklyn high school was exciting and challenging since some of the scenarios could have been depicted in the movie *Blackboard Jungle* with Sidney Poitier. Upon graduation, I became a proud and eager licensed teacher.

Who would have imagined that the obligation to become an educator for the student loan for the year abroad in Spain would pave the way to one of my greatest passions!

Thank you, Queens College, for the memories and opportunities of a lifetime. I'll never forget you nor the magic of studying abroad in España at the Universidad de Granada, La Facultad de Filosofía y Letras.

Vera, selected as Miss Foreigner, is serenaded by the Tuna, 1967. Photo by a fellow student.

Flamenco's Cultural Roots

IF YOU'VE EVER listened to the haunting strains of flamenco and heard what you believe are Jewish connections, you are right.

According to one theory, flamenco has deep Jewish roots in addition to Indian, Greek, Roman, and Persian influences; it is surmised that the flamenco art forms were brought to Spain by Gypsies who traveled from northwest India to Pakistan and Persia into fourteenth-century and fifteenth-century Europe and into Andalucia in southern Spain. Some historians say the music's debut might have been as early as 711 CE, brought by Arab armies coming from North Africa. Andalusian music is an amalgam of Arabic music with Hindu, Greek, Hebrew, and Persian influences. Local folk music and dances date back to Phoenician and Roman times.

Flamenco became a voice of protest of dissenting Christians, Muslims, Jews, and other "outcasts" who didn't fit into the new political order of Queen Isabella and King Ferdinand. Los Reyes Catolicos ended the harmonious coexistence among Muslims, Jews, and Christians after their capture of Granada from the Moros in 1492. Muslims and Jews were forced to convert to Christianity, and those who resisted were eventually expelled. Gypsies were forced to settle down and put an end to their nomadic lifestyle.

Further, after the 1492 Expulsion, a Jewish voice "resurfaced" in flamenco. The plaintive wailing of religious prayer, now forbidden, became the secular "aaiiee" of the conversos (Jews forced to convert to Christianity), with the notable exception of the Saeta. The Saeta sung today during Holy Week dates back centuries and is generally agreed to have Jewish origins. The conversos sang in their traditional manner but changed the words to demonstrate their devotion to their new Christian faith; singing, no doubt, with extra verve and passion to dispel any doubts of their sincerity. There are also strong similarities between certain synagogal chants and some early forms of cante flamenco.

The Peteneras form of flamenco is likely linked to Sephardim who settled in Turkey and other Middle Eastern countries.

According to the theory, the Peteneras was passed down through the generations since the 1492 exile. Another hint as to Peteneras' Jewish origins is that even today, many Gypsies refuse to sing or dance Peteneras and consider it unlucky. The music's status as unlucky may be rooted to the long history of persecution of the Sephardim.

It Was You!

*dedicated to my dearest junior and senior
high school friend, Susan Winnick*

It was you who led the way to my destiny.
It was you who asked me about plans after high school.
It was you who saw me as a college student.

Yes, you, who helped transform my passion for
languages into reality.
Yes, you led me to Don Quijote and España.
No one else but you!

Thank you.

An Ode to Sleep

dedicated to the "all nighters" while studying for exams

Oh, Alpha, Alpha
Lead me to slumber
That I may rest my restless soul!

How I crave thee,
My savior,
How I long to be whole!

Protecting my ego
Wears the flesh from the bone.

Is it morning yet?
Am I dreaming…
Or is it the phone?

España

You taught me Pleasure
You taught me Love
You gave me raison d'etre
I was free as a Dove.

You taught me Franco
You taught me Joy
You taught me Intolerance
Yet, I was free as a "Boy."

ESPAÑA…I fell in love with you and your people,
Your Prado, your tapas, your gitanos,
Your flamenco, your guitarras.

My Perfect Past

Living in Granada;
Speaking its native tongue;
Enjoying the Judeo-Christian-Arabic culture;
Studying the works of Cervantes.
This was my perfect past!

Chatting with students in the University,
Dancing flamenco as if I were a Gypsy
Dancing with my Latin lover.
That was my perfect past!

Walking through the streets of Toledo,
Seville, Málaga, Córdoba;
Entering the synagogues, churches, and mosques
made me feel like a child of all souls;
And that we were all One!
Blended together like the eclectic mix of tapas.
What glory!
How perfect was the past!

El Pasado Perfecto

Viviendo en Granada;
Hablando castellano;
Gozando de la cultura judía, cristiana y árabe;
Estudiando Cervantes
¡Eso fue el pasado perfecto!

Charlando con los estudiantes universitarios;
Bailando flamenco como si fuera gitana;
Bailando con mi novio.
¡Eso fue el pasado perfecto!

Andando por las calles de Toledo, Sevilla, Málaga, y Córdoba;
Entrando dentro de las sinagogas, iglesias, y mezquitas
me hizo sentir como hija de todos almas.
¡Y que éramos UNO!
¡Igual como mezclando tapas de todos tipos!
¡Ay! ¡Qué maravilla!
¡Qué perfecto fue el pasado!

There Was a Time She Felt Alive!

There was a time she felt alive,
Standing high up amongst the clouds.
The land of Cervantes, Quijote, and Sancho
Enticed her to stay.
Was not her soul here centuries ago?

Embers, remnants
of yesteryears' passions:
Flamenco cantantes singing to the depths of her bosom
As if she had never left.
There was a time she felt alive!

El Generalife's manicured cypresses reaching to the heavens;
Its grapevines, rose bushes, and its fragrances;
The Moorish fountains, arched windows, and
tiles of the 1300's,
Were now her treasures.
There was a time she felt alive!

The Alhambra with its jeweled, honeycomb stalactite ceilings,
Arabesque carvings around its windows;
Pools reflecting 14th-century arched porticos.
Canopies with stonework in the Lions' Courtyard.
There was a time she felt alive!

Tapas of mussels, shrimp, and clams
With their slimy textures;
The hard Granadine cobblestone streets;
Brought me back to reality.
There was a time I felt alive!

Había una Vez Que Se Sintió Viva

Había una vez que se sintió viva,
De pie en lo alto entre las nubes.
La tierra de Cervantes, Quijote y Sancho
La atrajo para que se quedara.
¿No estaba su alma aquí hace siglos?

Ascuas, restos de las pasiones de antaño:
Cantantes flamencos cantando a lo más profundo de su seno
Como si nunca se hubiera salido.

Los cipreses bien cuidados del Generalife,
alcanzando a los cielos;
Sus vides, rosales y sus fragancias;
Las fuentes moriscas, ventanas arqueadas y
azulejos de los años 1300,
Ahora eran su tesoro.
¡Había una vez que se sintió viva!

La Alhambra con sus techos de joya,
Tallas arabescas alrededor de sus ventanas.
Piscinas que reflejan pórticos arqueados del siglo XIV
Toldos con mampostería en el patio de los Leones.
¡Había una vez que se sintió viva!

Tapas de mejillones, gambas, almejas
Con sus texturas viscosas;
Las duras calles empedradas granadinas;
Me trajo de vuelta a la realidad.
¡Había una vez que yo me sentí viva!

And She Smiled

Her blood-stained birthplace became hostile to Diversity.
At age two, she left on the *Radnik*, in
which she nearly drowned;
And she smiled.

The new warring "promised land" welcomed the little refugee
in a shack till she was six;
And she smiled.

America welcomed the six-year-old "miracle" child;
The land of Freedom offered
Dreams to be explored and Discoveries to be made.
And she smiled.

Her Dad's Nightmares awakened the young heart;
She comforted him.
And she smiled.

America offered her a new language and education.
Knowledge lavished upon her self-respect and
respect from others;
And she smiled.

Literacy spread her wings to University;
To Franco's Valley of the Fallen,
Where she succumbed to the heavens.
And she smiled.

Named Miss Foreigner & serenaded by "la Tuna,"
She breathed in the soul of the Andalucian textures,
As if her spirit had been there before.
And she smiled.

He was lean and Latin.
His dark sunglasses reflected the chestnut mestizo eyes.
His glances pierced her groin
And she was transformed from youth to woman.
And she smiled.

Then reality:
You're not Catholic? You're not Protestant? What are you?
A classmate inquired.
And she smiled.

Marriage beckoned:
Her "Rock of Gibraltar" she did wed,
Followed by her two precious gems;
Her career goals unmet.
And she smiled.

Society's wrongs, "Doña Quijote" wanted to right;
Respect for Diversity became her mantra.
She fought for "green air" and celebrated teens.
And she smiled.

Today, her gray hair blows in the wind;
Wiser? Oh, Yes!
She always tries to think, speak, listen, and validate with Love.
Oneness with All!
And she smiles.

Returning to the Land of Sancho and Quijote[9]

My Dream Vacation

Fifty-four years I waited,
to return to the land of Sancho and Quijote.
I was ready to leave this May,
until COVID's unwelcome visit left me dismayed.

Had I been there in May,
would I have still been hugged by my ancestors' clouds?
At the peak of the Valley of the Fallen,
like I had been cuddled then?

Would I have still felt the heartbeat of the canto hondo
and danced as if my feet were blazing with
the fire of the Gitano?
Would I have visited the Roma
in the whitewashed caves of Sacromonte,
as I did back then?

Or would I have just sat back in awe,
smiling, and grateful
that I lived there then?

Breath & Visualization Exercise

Let's begin with a brief relaxation exercise
and, preferably, close your eyes gently, if you wish.

Breathe out stress and stiffness;
Breathe in relaxation and resilience.

Breathe out all future worries and concerns;
Breathe in the peaceful, present moment.

Breathe out any resistance;
Breathe in acceptance of what is.

Now, envision yourself at your favorite place.
What sights do you see?
What sounds do you hear?
What fragrances or smells do you smell?
What tastes do you taste?

Imagine something or someone whispering in your ear and asking you, *Who are you?*

And as you gently begin to open your eyes, *take a minute or two, to reflect, write, or create a graphic about who you are.*

Planting Seeds for Your Story

Getting to Know You, Your Feelings, Your Emotions, Your Thoughts

1. Select one poem that resonates or connects with your heart and soul.
2. Ask yourself:

    - Why did I select this poem?
    - What does it remind me of? What happened? What feelings arose?
    - Who was involved?
    - Where did this occur?
    - When did it happen?

3. Express your story in any format by writing a poem, essay, play, novel, or lyrics to a song, sketching, drawing, photographing, or making a video.

    - Who were you in the past?
    - Who did you become?
    - Who are you today?
    - Did anyone or anything have an impact or influence on you that might have contributed to who you were, became, or are today?
    - How can you use your story for social change?

4. Did you discover any new revelations from telling your story? Did it resolve any issues? Did you share it with another?
5. How did you feel upon completing your story? Write for three pages, without stopping, without any concern for spelling or grammar.

Chapter Three: Marriage & Children

Vera, lower right; Genene, top right; Marty, top left; Garrin, lower left, in a restaurant in Boca Raton, Florida. Photo by a server.

Introduction:
Marriage:
Serendipity

I TRULY BELIEVE that the best things and people come into our lives unexpectedly, without our planning. And great rewards can come when one surrenders with acceptance rather than resistance.

As a senior in college, I had a roommate who practically begged me to join her at a club in NYC one evening. I resisted because I was studying for midterms and really wasn't in the mood to go. I finally gave in and went.

Soon after we entered Wednesdays, a dance club, an attractive young man approached me and asked me to dance. Well, that handsome young man became my fiancé months later. I remember inviting him to meet my parents in South Plainfield, New Jersey, for dinner.

I was so accustomed to speaking in Hungarian to my parents that I introduced my date in English and then proceeded to speak to them in my native tongue; it was the language I spoke since I could say, "*anyu es apu*" (Mommy and Daddy) and old enough to ask, "*Hogy vagy?*" or "How are you?" It came so automatically, and eventually my date reminded me that he didn't understand Hungarian and to please speak English.

Soon, we sat down to dinner and my mom, proudly, served Marty a big bowl of soup consisting of chicken, matzo balls, carrots, celery, cauliflower, parsnips, potatoes…every vegetable imaginable! Marty loved it and whispered in my ear, "What's next?"

I replied, "That's the dinner."

My 170-pound, muscled hunk was used to the typical steak and potatoes. Thankfully, Mom had also made a traditional dessert called palacsinta, similar to the French crêpe, filled with almond paste and fruit. And Marty enjoyed it!

We dated less than a year, and he proposed on New Year's Eve, 1968; we married on May 4, 1969.

The Child in You

"What's the squiggly green thing on our screen?" I asked.

"It's a caterpillar," he replied.

"Put it outside...no pupae here, please." So he went to get a covered glass jar, leaves, and water.

"Nature is incredible," he murmured. "The variety of organisms...The millennium of evolutions" and...

"Look at the yellow baby ducks and the little dark one," he said in amazement, sitting on our patio one morning, eyes wide open with a big smile, like a child's.

"Yeah, it reminds me of the Ugly Duckling," I answered.

"Look how the father duck trails behind the mother and the babies. He stays behind, ready to protect."

"How can you tell which is the male or the female?" I asked naively.

"The male is bigger and is the protector," he replied in his proud macho voice.

"Oh, of course, you're right, honey." I agreed, not in the mood to argue.

"Have you seen those little baby red birds in their nest in our tree near the bedroom yet?" he asked with excitement. "They sleep there at night while the mother and father fly away and return in the morning," he said convincingly, as if he were watching them day and night.

And another time, he described his encounter with a squirrel: "I was walking in our backyard and heard a squirrel making noises; so I decided to answer him trying to emulate the same sounds. Quickly, he perked up his ears and tiptoed towards me and repeated the same sounds as if he was conversing with me. This went on for a few seconds. How could anyone tell me that animals have no personality or soul?"

It was too early for me to get into a whole philosophical, controversial topic, so I just listened with admiration as I ate my breakfast.

Haiku

The moonlight brightens;
Your voice soothes, I surrender;
Light shines in my heart.

The ocean glistens.
Water surrounds all around.
You speak and I smile.

Why Do I Love?

Why do I love?
Love makes me see your shining soul.

Why do I love?
Love makes me hear your heart's truth.

Why do I love?
Love beckons me to reach out to you.

Why do I love?
Love creates memorable memories.

How do I love?
Without expectations.

How do I love?
Validating your truths.

How do I love?
Listening to you in the present moment.

How do I love?
Watching you smile at the blooming pink and white
Bougainvilleas that you nurtured and nourished.

I See…

I see God's Eyes
In the light of the Sabbath candles.

I see God's Eyes,
In your eyes, dear husband, dear daughter, dear son.

I see God's Eyes
In everyone.

Motherhood

Twelve months after we were married, my first beautiful gem, our daughter, was born, and eighteen months later, our handsome son. It wasn't until many years later that I realized how much I had learned from my children, and I really wasn't ready to "get it" until they became young adults. I wish we'd been offered "Parenting 101." Perhaps, I would have been more aware of why our precious daughter had the occasional habit of slamming her bedroom door.

Genene was the sweetest—a trouble-free, quiet child, seemingly content. She loved her playpen; by two, she really started rebelling against shoes, designer clothes. She seemed to know what she wanted. She wanted to learn to ride a tricycle her way, barefoot, until my uncle Martin helped her realize that shoes were a better fit for riding. Genene was so cute with her rosy cheeks in the adorable dresses my mom loved to buy her, especially the sun dresses in the summer months! And she really enjoyed laughing and running around our backyard with her friends.

Garrin had allergies and was irritable, especially when he drank milk, until I realized that he needed a different formula; this seemed to ease his crankiness.

Then our pediatrician, Dr. Seda Morales, felt he needed to have casts placed on each of his legs to straighten them out more; I only wish someone would have thought of simple massaging. I felt so sad for him, especially when the casts were removed with that noisy tool that prompted our sweet baby boy to cry and scream from the sound.

As he got into his twos, our adventurous son loved to watch *Batman* on tv and started carrying on, running in circles around the barely furnished living room with his cape and mask. He was really cute, though he got a bit too rambunctious, and I said, "Okay, no more Batman for you." In his quieter time, he loved to place pennies in between the keys on our newly gifted upright piano, from his aunt Maureen's parents.

Blessings In Disguise

"My son, no more Batman for you…too much violence."
"Daughter dear, walking barefoot isn't safe,
Please wear shoes for your mother's sake."

"My son, what's with pennies, dimes between piano keys?
Are these for me, you, or your big sis?"

"Daughter dear, do you have allergies to washing dishes?"
"But, Mom, doing my homework, that's one of my wishes."

Mom used to say, "You give them a finger,
they'll want the hand."

I must admit the older they got
The prouder I became:
Their kindness, their kisses!
Their music, their band!

I loved their "hits"
And forgave their "misses"!

Remember, Garrin?

Hess trucks
Hess cars
Hess planes.

Remember, Garrin?
Receiving these toys,
during Hanukkah each year
when you were my little boy?

The long red one with flashing lights and sounds of a horn,
an engine starting and gear reversing?

And the one with its motorized tractor and
swiveling brackets
and the truck with the super jet plane
on board?

What great memories to watch my boy
play and enjoy!

Remember, Genene?

Remember New Jersey, Genene?
Turkey Swamp Park?
Swinging round and round on the carousel.
And Sandy Hook Beach,
with you and Garrin shelling?
And Marlboro Brook,
finding sharks' teeth while fossiling?

TOGETHER
Remember Spanish class?
¿Cómo estás? And *Me llamo*.
And Young Authors;
writing your original stories in your sewn books?
And the Village School,
creating a volcano that overflowed with lava of
vinegar and baking soda.

TOGETHER
Remember, Genene?
Working on *The Kids' Press*,
and your poem, "Fun" at age seven;
your artwork and Garrin's for "Dear Doc Bubbles"
about children with troubles;
your drawings of a little goat and kitty cat for an
eleven-year-old's story
and her feeling sorry for her pets.
And Garrin selling *The Kids' Press*
at teachers' conventions in
Atlantic City?

TOGETHER
Remember?

Children's Creativity Day at Monmouth Mall?
Your award-winning story was not the end all!
Your fluting and tooting; and Garrin, drumming
with the Temple Shalom Band,
made great music for seniors at hand.

For the Love of Music

Mom had introduced me to the love of music when she insisted that I learn to play the accordion, which was popular in Europe but not with me. Her influence on my passion for music resurfaced when my own children were in elementary school and I, too, insisted that they play an instrument. The major difference was that I encouraged my daughter and son to try different ones, such as the piano, to begin.

Garrin played the drums initially, and since we were concerned with possible hearing loss, we encouraged him to select another instrument; he chose the guitar, which he still plays today. My daughter chose the flute and performed it in the school orchestra for about eight years.

To ensure that they practiced, I learned to be a conductor and created an orchestra of young musicians at our temple; we all enjoyed volunteering and playing at nursing homes and at malls during holidays. It was a win-win for the temple, the youngsters, their parents, and my family.

Both my children had a love and great ear for music; Genene enjoyed singing and eventually sang in school plays and at the school "coffee house." Garrin was able to play whatever he heard on the radio or his cassette tapes. He did learn to read music, though he preferred just listening to his favorite songs and then playing them by ear.

In high school, they were both very active in talent shows and won many of them, together and individually. Hearing and seeing them on stage melted my heart with pride and so much joy. Genene performed as Tzeitel in *Fiddler on the Roof* at Spanish River Community High School. During this time, she wrote many poems and often set them to music. Many years later, she performed her original songs such as "Love Remains" and "Make Me Happy," sometimes with Garrin's musical accompaniment, in venues in New Jersey and New York. Lyrics for a few of her songs appear later in this chapter.

After college, where Genene majored in journalism and communication, she chose to become an editor and, in fact, edited one of my first award-winning books, *Teens Are Heroes, Too! Challenges, Choices and Character*. She was also a writer, songwriter, proofreader, and editor for publishers, magazines, and newspapers such as the *Sun Sentinel*.

Garrin majored in sociology and eventually became a digital marketing whiz for major companies and eventually his own. Through one of his clients, he had the opportunity to network with sports teams and helped Genene fulfill her passion for singing by arranging for her to sing the national anthem on ice at the Huntsville, Alabama, hockey arena in front of three thousand spectators. Tears fell lovingly and proudly from my eyes as she belted out one of the most meaningful songs in my life, given my roots as a naturalized citizen. Once again, I was so proud of both of them.

And Marty, I was proud of you!

Happy Father's Day…

To my friend and my lover;
a husband and a father like no other.

Whether boating with Garrin,
or gardening with Genene,
you've always been there
in all kinds of scenes.

Attending their concerts and
going on trips;
researching their issues
and dealing with hardships.

We could always depend on
your love and friendship;
your companionship
and even an occasional ego trip!

In all kinds of weather,
we'll love you forever.
Today on Father's Day,
Let's enjoy our day together!

Your Essence, My Daughter

Stillness is your essence, my daughter.
Stillness was your message
While still in my womb.
Your stillness quieted
My restless Soul;
It gave me peace and self-control.

Your angelic, porcelain face;
Your softness,
Calmed and soothed.

I Celebrate Your Birth!

Genene (right) and Vera (left). Photo by Marty Hirschhorn.

The Love of a Child

In my 40s I had a crisis:
Fear overwhelmed me,
Weakness ensued.
Immobile physically,
Alert mentally,
Emotionally drained
Forced into Stillness.

My soul needed love;
I wanted attention,
His attention!
I wasn't fulfilled,
Ego ruled me:
With all its negativities
Anger, jealousies, loneliness.

Mummified, numb, spiritless
I withdrew
No people,
No noise
I lived in a cocoon.

The love of a son who honored me,
And amused me
With games & music
Enriched my spirit!

Look at your parents, a loved one advised.
Did they give up & wither away?
Feel their Strength
And Choose to Live!

And so, I chose to live!

I'm So Grateful You're My Son

I admire how you transform vinegar into honey
no matter the issue, no matter the test.

I've always watched how you did your best:

Whether new careers, new home, or your gallbladder,
You've always persisted in climbing the ladder.

Always researching for solutions
You courageously draw good conclusions.

I've always taken pleasure in your passions and compassion
Expressed to me and others in Garrin-style fashion.

Your creative spirit guitaring, painting, dancing,
Photographing or sketching,
I enjoy the fact that you're never *kvetching*.

Your sense of humor and *joie de vivre*
Are an inspiration;
As is your adventurous spirit, for emulation.

Life is like a roller coaster
Changing through the years,
Sometimes smiles and sometimes tears.

During Grandma's Shiva
You recorded survival lessons that Grandpa taught
And helped him stay distracted instead of distraught.

Forever, I'll be grateful.

Vera (left) and Garrin (right). Photo by Garrin Hirschhorn.

I'm So Grateful You're My Daughter

Daughter, you've given me many blessings
And even some lessons.
Was it God's will
That we walk low valleys and climb many hills?

Sometimes the road was wobbly;
Often very steady;
And today, I'm ready,
To say, "I love you more than ever!"

You empathized upon hearing of my cataracts:
　"I'm so sorry, Mom."

You soothed my soul upon Grandma's passing:
"Mom, Grandma Judy's telling me she's okay;
So, don't worry."

You initiated research on my courageous Uncle Imre.

You eulogized Grandma Bertha unlike any other.
And sympathized as you drove me to a dear
friend's son's funeral.

And while we were away on high seas,
You flew to New York with your brother to pay family respects
at my cousin's Shiva.

Throughout your school years and to this very day,
Your voice, your lyrics have given me joy;
Not to mention the "Star Spangled Banner" you sang,
For thousands of men, women, girls, and boys!

And who could forget the surprises on Mother's Day?
Whether Sunday brunch at Cinemark, the
Norton, or Flagler Museum.
And sweet poems or cuddly bears for birthdays in May.

Genene, I love you forever!

What My Kids Have Taught

To listen more;
Preach less.

Validate, empathize more;
Philosophize less.

Trust more;
Question and Control less.

Express needs;
Expect less.

Accept what I can't change;
Change what I can.

Simply,
Hug
And love more.

My Greatest Teachers

"I'll always be a student," I remember thinking during my senior year in college. And now, many years later, I realize how true that's been throughout my personal, social, professional, and spiritual life.

During the "self-help" movement, I was digesting the books of Louise Hay, Deepak Chopra, Eckhart Tolle, Wayne Dyer, Anthony Robbins, and other motivational gurus. I was sticking memos with affirmations on my walls, my mirrors, everywhere to remind myself of their teachings. And then there were those who insisted that we were perfect just the way we were.

As children, we develop habits due to our perceptions and our family's dynamics, and as we get older, we realize that they no longer serve us. And how ironic that what serves us for a healthy relationship with ourselves and others has been taught by our very own children.

Yes, as a parent, I am very aware that I've made unintended, unconscious mistakes, as every parent and every human being makes. During the hills and valleys of times together with my own children, I've learned about the importance of validating their truth without offering unsolicited solutions nor defending myself nor interrupting them; that is, actively listening with both ears and zipping my mouth.

Thank you both!

Genene's Letter

Thank you, Genene, for your loving letter to my mom.

GRANDMA JUDY,

As your first grandchild, I have many fond memories of special times with you. I always felt safe and loved by you. Memories will always fill my heart and mind of things like the white boots you bought for me as a child and loved so much, the little blue and pink plastic cups you and Grandpa reserved for Garrin and me at your house in South Plainfield; Fluffy, your white poodle; the *Grease* album you and Grandpa gave me. Laughs and good times watching TV shows like *Different Strokes*, *Jeffersons*, *Good Times*, Archie Bunker and *Carol Burnett* and for you, *The Golden Girls* and *Who's The Boss?*; toys and games and dolls that you were so happy to give me; playing card games like War in Freehold, and coloring; looking through family photos.

I remember putting your make-up on your styrofoam head-shaped wig-holders and also the big blond-haired doll with the pink velvet dress and a barrette in her hair in Mommy's room; sleeping in Mommy's pink room and Uncle Hank's room; Chanukah presents; matzo ball soup, so yummy that we used to fight over it; playing in your Freehold back yard on the swing set; the orange vinyl chairs downstairs and Grandpa's big comfy recliner chair; your records like *Love Me Tender*.

In Florida, Garrin and I remember how you loved to hear me sing and Garrin play guitar. Garrin enjoyed talking to you about how you wanted him to meet blue-eyed "blondies." I also loved talking with you about your childhood and family: your oldest sister, Montsi, and how she used to stay up all night reading like I do; what you wore; how pretty you were as a girl and smart with your math skills; how you went to soccer games with your friends. I enjoyed sharing common interests with you—the color lilac, boys who play soccer, and little miniature chotchkas [sic] you always gave me which I will treasure forever. Of course, I always felt good hearing your advice about dating and boyfriends, too.

Grandma Judy, we remember your cute Hungarian and Yiddish phrases that Garrin and I always wanted to understand; your sense of humor, your laugh and your smile. Most of all, we remember your everlasting love and kindness, friendliness and generosity to me, my friends, and the whole family. You gave us, your grandchildren, all that we could ever want or need. We are very lucky to have had a grandma like you. We know how much you love us and we love you just the same with all our heart.

I love you, Grandma Judy, always have and always will. And remember, you are my sweetheart too!

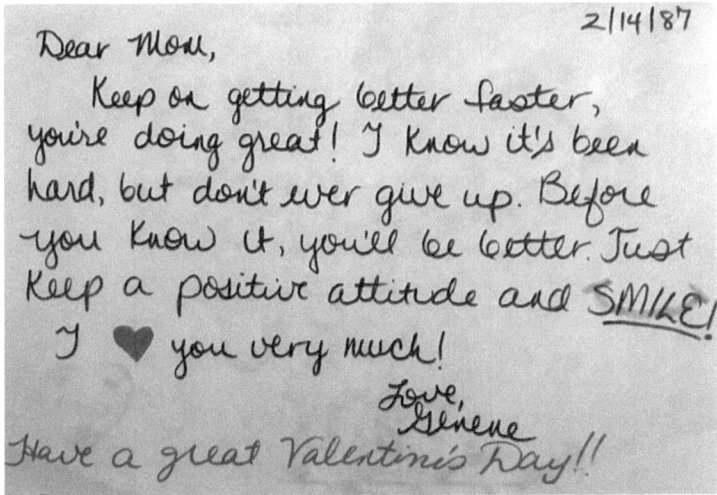

Valentine's card from Genene to Vera, 1987.

Garrin's Poem

Age 7, Grade 1
Village School, Holmdel

Living in a fish tank

I am a neon fish.
If I were a fish living in a tank
I would feel embarrassed.
Everybody would look at me.
People would think I was funny especially when they
would see me making faces.

I like this fish tank because I like sucking on the
thermometer. It tastes good!
When it changes temperature
I like looking at it.

I hide behind plants.
I like scaring the other fish
when I come out of the plants.
I like jumping up.

When somebody puts their finger in the water,
I think
it's food and I eat it.
It tastes yucky!

It is fun when I swim.

Garrin's Letters

*Thank you, Garrin, for following your heart
and passion for the environment.*

GARRIN HAS ALWAYS been very passionate and concerned about saving our earth. As early as age eight, he began writing letters to government officials about pollution in New Jersey and the need to clean up the air.

Garrin corresponded with New Jersey Governors Thomas H. Kean and Brendan Byrne in the early 1980's regarding pollution issues, and in response, they pledged to continue to study and propose solutions as well as to make the public aware of the necessity of protecting the environment.

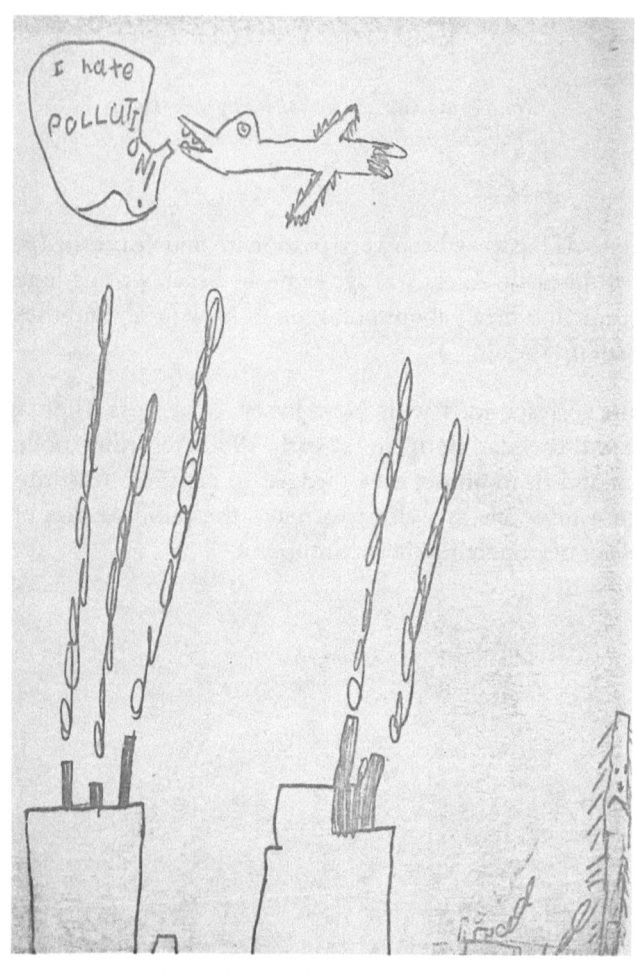

"I Hate Pollution." Drawing by Garrin Hirschhorn, age eight.

Another of Garrin's early letters was to a museum director in 1978 in which he expressed his observation about a "sea monster" found in New Jersey; the director's reply explained that it was probably a decomposed or partially decomposed whale, which can usually be identified from the skeleton. However, he continued, in this case all that was available to experts was a photograph from which important details were obscured. The director sent him a complimentary copy of *Sea Frontiers* magazine that included articles on strange animals in the oceans and suggested that Garrin subscribe.

At age fourteen, he wrote to Senator Al Gore regarding concerns about music censorship by the Parents' Music Resource Center, citing the First Amendment of the Bill of Rights and pointing out that the government was restricting citizens' rights by unfairly labeling available music. He argued that parents, not the government, were responsible for determining what their children should be able to listen to. Gore responded in defense of the policy, arguing that it was an issue of consumer information, public awareness, and truth-in-packaging and did not infringe on peoples' rights. He said that corporations had an obligation to inform consumers of content by labeling and lyric printing to serve as a tool to help parents exercise their responsibility and make informed decisions.

In the early 1990s, Garrin wrote to his senator regarding the availability of dietary supplements and concerns with the Food and Drug Administration's enforcement of regulations rather than allowing consumers to make their own informed decisions.

Even today, Garrin, still writes to officials about his concerns regarding the environment, such as the quality of water, for the well-being of his community.

Genene's Songs

Thank you, Genene, for these poems which you set to music that I love to sing and share with everyone.

Make Me Happy

Words and music by Genene Hirschhorn
Copyright 1995-2001 by Genene Hirschhorn. All rights reserved.

In the crisp cold air I saw you there,
Broken hardness, softened stares
Nothing beats the blue skyline
The blades of grass look sharp
But feel fine.

There is so much stimuli
But take me over, I'll let this kind
Reach me
Fill me
Make me happy
I'm so happy

The strumming lulls me to my knees,
To my feet,
It's so easy, it's so complete,
Let the air wash over me
I know I can make you happy
I know I can trust you, lovely

Sunbeams bounce around till dusk
Time to go but I'm in no rush.
Time to go but I'm in no rush,
Time to go but I'm in no rush.

Just make me happy,
I'm so happy,
Make me happy,
I'm so happy.

You in My Dreams

Lyrics by Genene Hirschhorn, Music by Garrin & Genene Hirschhorn
Copyright 1995-2002 by Genene Hirschhorn. All rights reserved.

VERSE
I close my eyes
I think of how it could be
With you in my dreams
Right here, close next to me

PRE-CHORUS
Where are you now
Where can I find you?
I ask myself how
How can I find someone true
Like you, in my dreams

CHORUS
You in my dreams,
Come alive for me,
You (you) you in my dreams
Be real to me

VERSE
I feel like you're the only one
Who could ever mean something to me
I want to meet you darlin'
But will you ever be?

VERSE
My heart is like a cave
So empty and alone
Don't you know I need you, babe,

Why can't you be my own?

BRIDGE
I'm callin' out to you
But will you ever hear?
I'm cryin out for you
Why can't you just be here?

GUITAR SOLO

CHORUS REPEAT

Soulmate

Words and music by Genene Hirschhorn
Copyright 1992-2003 by Genene Hirschhorn. All rights reserved.

(hi-hat at 56 bpm, Starting note=B)

VERSE
Lying on the mattress
Head in hand I gaze
Focusing on the curtain
Filtering sun into pink haze
My lips can almost feel you
They move forth anticipating
Overcome by thoughts of you
Everlasting waiting.

PRE-CHORUS
In a flash you are reality,
Then you fade away.
I really see us happening,
Then doubt brings back dismay.

CHORUS
Lover, lover
See as I
I'm for you
You can't deny.
Souls together,
Years apart,
You never really left me
You never really left me.

VERSE
Angels tell me all the time
Of how we lost each other.
And now they say the time is right,
Our love we shall recover.

CHORUS
Lover, lover
See as I
I'm for you
You can't deny.
Souls together,
Years apart,
You never really left me

You never really left me. >STOP HI-HAT HERE

OUTRO
Ya never really left me (babe)
You never really left me.

Love Remains

*Lyrics by Genene Hirschhorn, Music by Genene
Hirschhorn & Garrin Hirschhorn
Copyright 2001-2003 by Genene Hirschhorn & Garrin Hirschhorn.
All rights reserved.*

Darkness, darkness overtakes me
Night and day my mind forsakes me
Hope and love arise again
Till fear alone becomes my friend
Till fear alone becomes my friend.

This time, this time
I feel strong
Till anxious feelings come along.
Maybe there's a way to change
So this time only love remains,
So this time only love remains.

CHORUS
So much I want to get rid of the fear
And so much I want peace but it ain't here.
One full day not perceiving danger.
Let love remain and
make fear the stranger.

Sometimes when I look at you
I'm so scared that I don't know what to do.
If I could see beyond your face,
Maybe I could leave this place
And maybe fear could erase
And maybe you I could embrace

This time, this time
I feel strong
And anxious feelings,
well they don't come along,
'Cause I believe, I have my faith
That in me lies a better way, that
In me only love remains.

CHORUS
So much I want to get rid of the fear
And so much I want peace but It ain't here.
One full day not perceiving danger
Let love remain
and make fear the stranger.

GUITAR SOLO

So much I want to get rid of the fear
And so much I want peace but it ain't here.
One full day not perceiving danger,
Let love remain
and make fear the stranger.

One full day not perceiving danger
Let love remain and make fear the stranger
Oh. oh, oh
This time, love remains (2x)

Celebrating Our Love

Genene,
I'll always treasure

our tea time in West Palm Beach, the petit sandwiches and yummy scones.

how we looked at each other, laughing together at the movies of Shadowood.

our annual shopping trips at Lord & Taylor or Kohl's to celebrate your birthdays.

our talks about Old Testament stories. So thought-provoking!

when we visited Grandma Judy in the Broward Hospital during the semester you took off from the University of Florida. You were such a comfort during our drive.

how we sang your "Love Remains" and "Make Me Happy" at Grandma's eternal resting place, accompanied by your cassette tape. I'm sure she was smiling and listening with joy.

how we drove together on your search for a new apartment. Just being with you made me happy.

the fun time we shared at your new home, laughing and dancing non-stop.

our exchanges of "I love you."

Eulogy for Genene Gila Hirschhorn, 1970-2023

Your gifts were plenty:
You showed strength
And shined your light when mine was dimmed

You taught me to live life without regrets
And with purpose;
Because there's no turning back.

These last six months together, Genene,
were treasures:
Hugging and loving daily,
Forgiving each other,
And connecting our souls.

"Mom, you did the best you could"
"We all did the best we could"
Were words of blessings
Amidst tears of pain and joy.

You, Lisa, and me singing, "Three Little Birds"
Was truly divine!

Cooking together,
Eating together,
Holding each other's hands,
Walking together;
Unforgettable!

You fought the best fight
My Queen Esther,
My Courageous Champ.

Your strength endured
Right to the end!

And now your loving soul
Has ascended and is embraced by God
Now and evermore.

I love you forever
MOM

Connecting Soul to Soul

"Genene, what do you think?" I asked my precious daughter's soul while trying to make a decision at my ophthalmologist's office soon after my consult over the month-long stye on my right eye lid.

"I suggest that it be lanced," and, "yes, it will probably be bruised for a few days, and I can't guarantee it won't have a scar," the eye doctor added.

While waiting for him to return from other patients, I decided to call and ask my son, who said, "Absolutely not." Then, I called my husband, and instead of getting him on the phone, the funeral director, Joe, answered, just like last week, even though I thought this call-forwarding issue from my husband's cell number was resolved.

In any case, I asked Joe if he thought I should have the eye stye lanced. He said, "Absolutely not."

My precious daughter's soul had answered through our family's funeral director, who agreed with my son; and I chose to cancel the procedure. I was happy, really happy for having reached out to my daughter, who had transitioned a few weeks before, on May 8, 2023.

The Everlasting Light

As the candle light faded for my Baby Girl
I hugged the glass with the candle;
And her inner light rekindled the candle's, brighter than before.
Each time I cuddled "her," the light reawakened.
With the dawning of the new day,
I realized,
Her light will always shine within, and around me.

How Do You Turn Grief into Gain?

I TRIED TO stay engaged with people, things, and places, while having continuous flashbacks of what I could have, should have, or would have done. And on her past two birthdays, I celebrated by sharing her favorite cake or cookies or key lime pie with people who have also lost an adult child or, more recently, with my instructor and women in the Silver Sneakers classes I joined this year.

Once the shock had long passed, I chose to try to remember the positive, memorable memories; what we did together, whether singing, dancing, tea time, or simply laughing or reading her heartfelt, hand-written greeting cards.

I began to focus on living in the present moment and staying connected to family and friends and colleagues; grateful that they were still in my life. I so very much appreciated them, their soothing words and warming hugs.

And when tears began to flow, out of nowhere, I had to remind myself that everything changes and that nothing nor anyone stays the same in life. I also had to remember self-care and my Baby Girl's blessings, "Mom, you did the best you could."

Looking at Genene's photos, I had to accept, tearfully, the reality that she may not be here physically, yet she lives on through me and with me nonetheless. From time to time, I decided to write to her in a journal gifted to me by a friend or speak to her, especially when lighting the memorial candles. And when I see a butterfly greeting me at my garden, especially on my recent birthday, I feel and believe it's Genene.

To lift my spirits, I created a scholarship in her honor and in her memory. Thankfully, the Music Therapy Department at the

University of Miami accepted the annual gift; I know that the recipients will benefit as well as their current and future patients. And through these empathetic, compassionate, and talented students, I know that my beloved daughter will live on eternally with her legacy of touching peoples' souls through them.

Breath & Visualization Exercise

Let's close our eyes, if you wish,
for a brief relaxation exercise

Let's breathe out tension and tightness.
And breathe in relaxation and resilience.

Let's breathe out all should'ves, could'ves,
and would'ves from the past.
And breathe in the peaceful, present moment.

Let's breathe out any future concerns and worries
And breathe in acceptance of what is with gratitude.

Let's visualize some people for whom you are grateful.
And now, visualize a few things for which you are grateful.
Lastly, visualize several places for which you are grateful.

Imagine expressing your gratitude to some of the people.
Why and how will you express it to each of them?
And now, when you are ready, open your eyes gently and smile.

Planting Seeds for Your Story

Getting to Know You, Your Feelings, Your Emotions, Your Thoughts

1. Select one poem that resonates or connects with your heart and soul.
2. Ask yourself:

    - Why did I select this poem?
    - What does it remind me of? What happened? What feelings arose?
    - Who was involved?
    - Where did this occur?
    - When did it happen?

3. Express your story in any format by writing a poem, essay, play, novel, or lyrics to a song, sketching, drawing, photographing, or making a video.

    - Who were you in the past?
    - Who did you become?
    - Who are you today?
    - Did anyone or anything have an impact or influence on you that might have contributed to who you were, became, or are today?
    - How can you use your story for social change?

4. Did you discover any new revelations from telling your story? Did it resolve any issues? Did you share it with another?
5. How did you feel upon completing your story? Write for three pages, without stopping, without any concern for spelling or grammar.

PART TWO:
Who I Became (Loving Me)

Chapter Four:
Passions:
Arts, Nature, Education

Music and nature collages by Vera Hirschhorn.

Introduction:
The Light between Us

"What's going on with me?" I questioned my husband, a 24/7 entrepreneur.

"I can't seem to move," I added amidst tears.

I was at a standstill, like my once shiny, silver, eagle-decorated Trans Am, running its high octane, almost on empty and eventually screeching to a halt.

I felt my life unraveling. I was uprooted like the oak tree in my backyard during a dark winter's Nor'easter.

"What's happening to my Doña Quijote?" he chuckled, thinking it might cheer me.

My inner child was finally getting the attention she craved! Since her childhood, she had parented her immigrant parents and continued to do so while she nurtured her two children and her husband who was busy creating his business. Adult Vera was also studying for a master's degree in human nutrition to learn about reversing familial genetic diseases such as polycystic kidney disease through lifestyle and dietary changes. As a teacher of Spanish and gifted/talented students, she immersed herself in creating county-wide convocations such as "Nutrition Against Disease" while righting the wrongs of society's injustices of harmful pesticides and even religious and ethnic intolerances.

Is it a wonder that little Vera had had enough? It was her turn to be nurtured and nourished! Little Vera had needed her adult, too!

Soon, my husband began to prepare meals. Mom came over to help clean, and my son awakened my creative spirit as he serenaded me on his guitar. Surprisingly and eventually, I found myself strumming and singing John Denver's "Take Me Home, Country Road" and creating greeting cards. Birthday and anniversary cards, Father's Day and Mother's Day cards exploded from within me like a volcano that had been dormant for hundreds of years. Poems with still life, landscapes, and seascapes on mini watercolor canvases flowed out.

Mini collages with roving, rolling eyes for jumping frogs and deer; pom poms for tails of squirrels, monkeys, and bunnies; shiny crystal beads for birds' eyes abounded. My huggable, cuddly, pudgy new "friends" all brought smiles to me once again.

Painful memories of dad's PTSD with nightly nightmares evoked many poems such as "I Am a Bubble" and "I'm a Kite." They transformed my pain into love letters to nature: "I Am a Duck," "I'm a River," "I Am a Bark," "I Am a Pine Needle."

As the dark months of winter slowly became bright months of spring and summer, and the dogwoods bloomed with gracious splendor, so, too, my innate cheerfulness returned.

Smelling the fragrance of the lilacs evoked my childhood's playfulness in my mother's garden similar to Proust's "Petites Madeleines."

Photographing nature's gifts helped me recall my blessings. And soon, I sang and strummed my six strings to Johnny Nash's "I Can See Clearly Now."

Gratitude journaling, deep breathing, mindfulness, and prayer became daily rituals.

Looking back, I realize how my painting, sketching, writing, and guitar playing all helped me let go of the past and of worrying about the future; they gave me one of the greatest gifts of all...to live in the sensory present moment.

Carpe diem became my mantra. Soon, my inner child hugged and kissed me with forgiveness. Its needs were fulfilled; my inner child was at peace! I realized that my midlife exhaustion was a blessing in disguise as it ignited my passion for the arts.

In my healing, I began to feel immense admiration and respect for my parents for their strength and resilience. Little by little, I began to feel a sense of liberation. Little by little, I began to open my heart and feel more love than fear. I wanted to give and express more love, affection, and appreciation to my husband, daughter, and son without feeling the need to have to protect or please them or the need for them to please me. I began the long journey to try to learn to trust in their ability to resolve their challenges and that they were perfectly capable of taking care of their needs, despite my perception that I needed to be everyone's caretaker.

> Healing is Wholeness:
> Releasing fears;
> Sharpening my senses;
> Seeing Life's Luminescence...
>
> Surrender to what is;
> Forgive what was;
> Love is Now,
> Now is Love.

Arts

My Garden, A Collage

Sandpaper, grains of sand, well raked.
Pieces of brown bark randomly shaped.
Butterflies, flowers, bromeliads that are fake.
Yet, inner peace, my keepsake.

A sky of yellow, red, titanium white, and cerulean blue;
Of tissue paper, paint, and lots of glue.

My son's photo of me, smiling and without maquillage;
Sweet memories, thanks to my collage.

Sounds of Music

Ekphrastic poem written while listening to a classical piece

Tears well up from the depths of my soul
I'm marching; where to? With whom?
Why? Where am I going?
Where will I end up? Will it be with you? Will I be alone?

Peace, Nirvana, Dance, Dancing the waltz;
Dancing at a ball like royalty in a palace;
All is right, calm, serene, paradise on earth
I'm so moved, so inspired
To fly, to go higher and higher
Higher into the heavens
Soaring endlessly, never stopping.

Flying, soaring
Waltzing, a palatial ball
Flying, soaring, breathless
Trapeze artist
A balancing act.

Dissonance, anger, fear
Choppiness, disturbances
Go away, leave me alone
Had enough
Enough, enough, enough!

Ode To…

Your black straps imprisoned my little body.
Your white and black keys and black buttons
Felt like icicles beneath my little fingers
I hated you!

As I grew older,
You grew with me.
Rarely did you leave me;
Yet, I was so eager to leave you!

How could someone like you offer a gift
That I'd always treasure?
The gift of song, of music, of dance;
The Gift of Life!

…My accordion

The Dance of Life

Perched on a Tiki Hut,
the black crow surrenders. Another has usurped his safe haven.

The usurper flies away and the usurpee resumes
his sacred space

UNTIL
the usurper begins the hut dance, de nouveau.

A Sensory Experience

Guitar and songs are so comforting;
Music, flowers calm
the nerves that are so fragile!

Light rain is pleasant at times
While walking quietly.
Snow, too, is relaxing.

Golden sun in the morning,
Fresh air in the night
Soothe, when you allow them to!

Nature

Nature

"I go to Nature to be soothed and healed and to have my senses put in tune once more."
-John Burroughs

Thou art my Muse;
My peace, my serenity.

My spirit soars
Like the seagulls in flight;
I am at one with them
As I am one with You.

My soul ascends
Where egrets and bluebirds rest;
Where I am one with them.
As I am one with You.

Oneness with You
Oneness with all.

Nowhere

I wish I could blend in with the seagulls in flight,
As they disappear to nowhere.

Like the frothy waves that beckon me
To join them and flow nowhere.

And be in another space and time
On an adventure to nowhere.

Where Have I Gone?

Yesterday I was a woman whose laughter
seemed to have waned.
Yesterday I allowed my cheerfulness to fade.

Where did I hide for the last few years?
Why did I disappear?

I WANT ME TO BE ME AND RETURN!
Like the flower, I want to be kissed each day
by the morning light;
And not allow myself to ever wither away.
I want to be reborn and return like the perennial,
with the warmth of May.

TODAY I RETURNED…
with
My joie de vivre,
My zest for life
My passions,
My purpose.

"Vinegar into Honey"

I dedicate this poem to honor the memory of my beloved grandmother, Maria Berger Rip, who perished courageously during the genocide of 1944 in Auschwitz. My dad told me, in my adolescence, that her favorite expression during difficult times was changing "vinegar into honey."

As I go for my walk tonight,
I want to release the "vinegar" from my spirit.
Sadness arises, and I realize
I'm on a path to nowhere.

Suddenly, a gentle breeze kisses my cheeks
and combs my hair.
Leaves of dancing trees whisper tenderly:
"Transform 'vinegar into honey.'"

My Rainbow

The sudden wind blew away
The wounds in my heart
And the turbulent high tides
Crushed and buried them that day.

My bitter tears
Became honeyed raindrops
which gave birth to my rainbow of many colors.

Drinking from the Poetry of Life

Every moment of every day I drink from the poetry of life.
In rain, sun, and wind.
My thirst is quenched from rivers and streams.

Florida's trees.
The balmy breeze.
The bright ball of light melts my troubles away.

The sounds of sanderlings ignite my senses.
My body sways and I begin my dances.
I am alive!

Springtime

It's the rebirth of nature
Of fruit
Of vegetables
Of flowers.

It's the rebirth
Of narcissus
Of perfumed lilacs
Of hyacinths.

It's the rebirth
Of the spirit
Of friendships
Of hope!

How lucky to have renewal
In order to correct the past
How lucky for our soul to experience growth
And move forward from spring to summer.

La Primavera

Es el renacer de la naturaleza
De las frutas
De los vegetales
De las flores.

Es el renacer
De los narcisos
De las lilas perfumadas
De los jacintos

Es el renacer
Del espíritu
De las amistades
De la esperanza!

Qué fortuna el renacimiento
Para corregir el pasado!
Qué fortuna el crecimiento
De nuestro alma
Desde la primavera hacia el verano.

The Sands of Time

HAIKU

Gifts were washed ashore.
The sun stares in wonderment
Grains of sand hug them.

        The glaring sun rays
        Capture letters in bottles,
        Cradled by the sand.

The gentle sands of time
Release, embrace a message
The sea looks on, on.

        Pines pray to heaven,
        Emerald jewels shimmer here;
        Day of her passing.

Today it's rainy;
Balmy breezes kiss my cheeks
And comb my aged hair.

        Leaves, branches, trees dance;
        Awakening me to me.
        The soft sunlight renews.

Nature Speaks...Man Interrupts

"Sway with me in the warm sunlight,"
gestures the blade of grass.
"Inhale my perfume," entices the gardenia.
"Come, drink sweet nectar with me," lures the monarch.

"Listen as I sing to you," persuades the bluebird and,
"Bathe with me in the morning dew."
"Soar higher and higher," tempts the eagle

I sit in deep reverie, and then I'm awoken:
"Mrs. Hirschhorn, you have a phone call."

The Baby Woodstorks in the Wetlands

The screeching of the recently born woodstorks
doesn't bother me,
here in the wetlands.

The oak trees and the lake with mangroves
make me feel calm
as if I were dreaming.

And yesterday's thoughts,
are already forgotten in this present moment.
I feel as if I were
in another world, without any pain;
without any challenges,
Just here,
Alone.

Las Cigüeñas Americanas en los Humedales

No me molestan los gritos
de los cigueñitos, recién nacidos;
aquí en los humedales.

Los robles, y el lago con manglares
me hacen sentir tranquila,
como si fuera yo soñando;

Y mis pensamientos de antes,
ya olvidados en este momento del presente.
Me siento como si fuera
en otro mundo, sin ningún dolor;
sin ningún desafío,
sola.

Fun in the Sun[10]

To breathe in the ocean air,
To dive into the wet white foam.
To roam, along the sandy pier.

"Should I fish or should I just peer?"
"Beer first," said a beachcomber,
"I'll have only one."
What fun it is, to be in the sun.

Surfers, braving the high tide waves.
Colorful umbrellas shading the haze.
Boats, some idle,
Others at full speed,
"Slow down! There might be manatees."

Music playing,
Palm Trees swaying
To Caribbean rhythms
One by one.
What fun it is, to be in the sun!

"Tennis anyone?"
"Golf, if you please."
"Seize the day,"
Our inner voice prays.

Gardening! A tropical pleasure.
How sensory! What a treasure!
Gardenias, hibiscus, bougainvilleas
Are just some,
Drinking in and delighting in the Florida sun!
Yes, we Egrets, see and hear all,
As we fly and have Fun in the Sun.

A Meditation[11]

(Save the Oceans)

I listen to the woosh of the sea.
I listen to my breath;
Oneness with thee,
As I breathe in,
And I breathe out.

Your waves come in,
Your waves go out.
They mesmerize;
They hypnotize;
I am at peace.

You lull me to sleep,
As if I'm in my mother's womb.
The warmth of the Gulf
blows balmy breezes my way.
It soothes and comforts my weary soul!

Then suddenly!

Awakened by the rapid beat of your rhythmic dance,
I realize, I could live here,

Eternally!

Una Meditación[12]

(Salva Los Océanos)

Escucho los sonidos del mar.
Escucho mi aliento;
Unidad contigo,
Mientras inhalo y exhalo.
Tus olas entran y salen.
Me mesmerizan e hipnotizan;
Estoy en Paz.

El calor del Golfo
Sopla brisas cálidas hacia mí,
Calmando y consolando a mi alma cansada.
Me meces en los brazos para dormir,
Como si estuviera en el vientre de mi madre.

De repente,
Despertado por el latido rápido de tu baile rítmico,
Me doy cuenta,
De que estoy viva, una vez más.

Podría vivir aquí eternamente.

Reflections of You

The storm in my heart
Is soothed by the calming sea.

The white flurries above offer hope for change.

Relics of your spirit
Abound in my thoughts.

As foreign tongues
Call me back to Now.

Returning to Me

Returning to the waters of the sea
is like returning to my mother's womb;
feeling safe and at home.

Swishing, swashing
like a child at play;
it's times like these
where I long to stay.

Here, I'm grounded
like the palm trees
around me;
that shade me
and feed me.

Here, like the endless horizon above,
I'm free
to be me.

Nature's Cure

Lying in the shade of a stranger's beach umbrella,
I rest my weary, wrung-out flesh
Near my white-breasted, grey-winged fella.

The salty air clears my sinuses;
I can breathe again!
Without the hacking, the choking, the gagging.

Nature's my cure!
Instead of man's synthetics,
Here, I've found relief with something pure.

O Strong, Sacred Rock

O strong, sacred rock!

Hug my needy sole
which yearns for your sun-kissed warmth and coral strength.

Embrace my flesh that longs to absorb your healing touch
as my feet stand firmly planted on your fossilized surface.

Teach me to flow, ocean sublime,
to aspire, to ascend
like the undulating foam before me.

Help me breathe in God's essence
to release the darkness from within
and let my soul mend.

The Ocean Breathes

While I lie awake at night,
the sounds of the ocean
bring my thoughts to the present.

The ocean waves remind me:
to breathe in,
to breathe out,
to breathe in,
to breathe out.

What a friend I have at night,
as the calming waves cradle me to sleep
and I
inhale,
ex...ha...le.
Inhale
ex...

My Companions at Sea

Boats on the horizon,
racing along.
Teeny bitsy buggies;
they don't belong.

A seagull's my companion;
Charley's my muse.
He runs with his sibling;
The sand's like a fuse.

Charley is chunky;
His brother is not!
Good Samaritans to their mom,
though the gritty grains are hot.

Such energy,
I've rarely seen.
They play tag and
Grandpa nags.

I just write while
the buggies bite.

I Only See a Child

I only see a child,
not a black child
nor a white child.

The child runs after
black/grey-tailed birds
and chases them into flight.

Smiling amidst the rushing waves;
She dances and splashes
In the transparent green waters.

As clouds of grey tones
warn of impending storms,
she still dances and splashes.

Her mother runs after her
And grasps her little arms,
beneath the "sparks of light."

I only see a child,
not a black child
nor a white child;

Only a child!

Hurricane Matthew

Dedicated to Farmer's Table Restaurant & Wyndham Hotel Boca Raton, Florida, who were there for me, Marty, Genene, Garrin, and the Boca Raton community

We'll always remember the night Matthew
was to visit.
Like little children, we huddled together,
fearing a monster lizard.

Then, like comforting parents,
you surprised us all:
you nourished our bodies
and nurtured our souls.

The steak, chicken, quinoa with lentils, salad, veggies,
to name just a few.
What a feast we had,
thanks to you!

Much gratitude for all your treats;
above all, your compassion, your caring
during the high winds, the rain and the Florida heat!

Hurricane, 2024

The pounding wind on my bedroom windows;
the rain, tap, tap, tapping;
the trees brushing by,
awoke me.

Switching the light on,
I was grateful;
soon, light flickered on, off
until it vanished.

A sandstorm arose;
the wind chasing the rain,
faster and faster,
more furious than ever.

Leaves of gold and crimson
rebelliously flying all over
and drifting wildly on my door.

Florida? No!
Blowing Rock, North Carolina's Helene!

The Dance of the Bonsai

Inspired at the Japanese gardens of the Morikami Museum

The foamy water rushing down the moss-covered rocks,
Cooling the sun-drenched pine trees behind them.
The clear waters of the lake
bathe the red, orange, and yellow dancing poi.

The bonsai nearby dance their unique story;
mini ficus, serapes, elms, tamarinds,
and wiandes *plient* to the left and *etendent* to the right.

Soon a grey-and-white-feathered egret sweeps by;
glides onto a coral boulder
and then darts into the sky once again,
dancing its own story.

Chimes in the breeze swing, sway, and sing;
humming their story,
each one a different note!

Trees Are People Too!

An olive tree once stood erect and tall
Like a soldier protecting a monarch's soul.
Then working boys played with destructive toys,
Shrieking, banging, knocking, chipping, chipping, chipping

Slowly the olive tree tilted;
No longer erect does the olive tree stand.
You see, builders killed its spirit and poise.
It couldn't take the ear-splitting noise.

He Made Eye Contact with Her

He made eye contact with her.
Their glances locked in a peaceful trance.
He moved closer and closer and closer,
Until their lips met.

Soon, they were totally intertwined, enveloped,
One within the other.
They passionately embraced from head to toe.
Gently! Heavenly!

Suddenly, a grayish figure emerged
and abruptly separated the two lovers;
Not an utterance was heard,
As they succumbed.

The intruder looked darker and darker,
As he completely overwhelmed them.
This is where the clouds bid their last adieu,
Never to see each other again.

Clouds

The orange moon rises among the black clouds,
Playing peek-a-boo.
How perfect for Halloween.

A dog transforms
Into a baby cub and squirrel.
The magic of clouds.

Painting clouds is painting life.
Black gouache, grey gesso, and
A palette of watercolors.
Ultramarine blue and alizarin crimson
draws me away from you;
Alizarin and quinacridone gold warms me towards you.

Change—It's Inevitable!

The pastel blue lake
Surrounded by snow-covered mountains;
Dark grey trees scattered all around the periphery.

Minutes later,
The lake transforms
And the snow-covered mountains are
An image of the past
As were the dark trees
Scattered here, scattered there.

All re-shapes, all re-forms;
Mountains become hills
Lakes become ponds
Light becomes dark,
Dark becomes light.

What the Mountains Teach

Life is precious;
enjoy each second, for deer can cross Teton Village Road
unexpectedly and Wham…!

Embrace the moment;
the view can change instantly.

Take one step at a time;
hiking up and down quickly to 7,000 feet is taxing.

Go slowly;
lack of O_2 can take your breath away.

Be flexible and acclimate;
mountain weather is unpredictable.

Be independent and self-sufficient;
isolation is commonplace.

Create your own magic,
with the beauty that abounds.

Celebrate diversity;
mountain peaks vary in shape, size, and height.

Respect earth's blessings;
bison, elk, moose, deer are all awesome!

Haiku

Ekphrastic poems based on a friend's abstract expressionist paintings

Morning Dew

Dancing in the dew
In purple, white, and gold haze;
Happy Days begin.

Windswept

Azures, crimsons, greens,
Autumn leaves are falling now,
Mother Nature Sings

Right Here, Right Now

Right now, right here is life
The sea is living
The algae is alive
The waves rushing in and out
The wind whistling.

Kids are swimming
Teens are eating
Kiddies are screaming.

Moms are resting
Families are gathering
Hugging, kissing and
Living, loving, and laughing.

And me, I'm just happy to be here,
Listening, watching, and enjoying
Right here, right now.

Education

Education

EDUCATION WAS ANOTHER important passion in my life.

While raising my children, I taught Spanish and flamenco dancing in adult schools at night to make ends meet since my husband had started his own business. Additionally, I created The Language Exchange, an interpreting/ translating service for attorneys. I was grateful to Marty, who recruited them, and I was thankful to the college students I called upon for requested languages such as Mandarin. I interpreted for legal depositions in Spanish and Hungarian when needed.

During the day, I began to publish *The Kids' Press* for, about, and by students, ages six through thirteen. I also edited their articles on science, sports, hobbies, music, poetry, movies, and books.

I wanted to give my daughter and son and all children a positive outlet for creative expression, as I always believed that every child is gifted in some way. My eight-year-old daughter and some of the older students helped me edit and proofread the publication. My daughter grew up to become a professional writer, copyeditor, and proofreader.

The first year of publication, my seven-year-old son sold many copies of *The Kids' Press* at the New Jersey Teachers' Convention in Atlantic City, where I gave workshops on *Students Acting as Professionals*. My son now uses his salesmanship in his own photography business, in addition to his marketing and technology skills.

I received subscriptions and submissions throughout that year and was happy to learn that *The Kids' Press* paved the way for many of the students to become professionals in relevant fields. One youngster, for example, became a professional cartoonist.

The only newspaper by and for kids at the time, *The Kids' Press* also led to Children's Creativity Day at a local mall. I invited over five hundred young professional elementary students to exhibit, demonstrate, or perform their talents, hobbies, and/or interests in the arts and sciences. This event also made the public aware of existing programs by teachers and schools in basic skills and creativity.

Teaching for Social Change

WHILE MY CHILDREN were in middle school, I returned to teaching as a full-time "gifted and talented" teacher and used the platform to create curriculum for social change. Aware that junk food was sold in schools, at work, and in all public places, I initiated a county-wide, two-day convocation entitled Nutrition Against Disease. I invited speakers like Dr. Lendon Smith, a pediatrician and author of many books such as *Foods for Healthy Kids* and *Improving Your Child's Behavior Chemistry*. Another workshop presenter, Rosalind La Roche, a recovered schizophrenic who founded and authored Earth House, attributed orthomolecular nutrition for freeing her from mental institutions.

Upon hearing the important role of healthy nutrition in healthy kids, teams of students were asked to solve the societal problem of healthcare: "Should the government enforce a law requiring all components of society to practice prevention of diseases?" A minimum of five components such as family, social service agencies, recreational agencies, physicians, schools, insurance companies, restaurants, and businesses had to be selected. They needed to decide to what degree the government should enforce such a law. Their plan had to be original and practical for possible implementation. Solutions were role played in "What If" scenarios based on the information they acquired from the myriad of speakers.

As a follow-up, my sixth and seventh grade students researched, interviewed, wrote, and acted in their five-minute film, *That's Inedible*, which was aired on television. Once again, students interacted with professionals, including those in the television industry.

Thanks to this convocation and with permission from the Board of Education, I initiated—along with my principal, the Food Services Director, and the Parent-Teacher Association (PTA)—a change in our school's lunch menu. Raisins, nuts, fruit juices, fresh fruits, and veggies replaced high-sugar and processed snacks. I also began workshops for colleagues state-wide that addressed the relationship between poor nutrition and depression, teen suicide, and juvenile delinquency.

The convocation inspired me to pursue a master's degree in Human Nutrition, and my thesis was entitled, *Pesticides in Food Can Be Dangerous to Our Health*. And so, I freelanced as an educational and nutritional consultant.

Volunteering

IN FLORIDA, WITH the arrival of many Russians who had been denied their freedom of religion and their civil rights, I chose to volunteer as an English for Speakers of Other Languages (ESOL) teacher in the School District of Palm Beach County to help immigrants eventually become naturalized citizens.

In gratitude for the successful cataract surgery I had at a very early age, I also volunteered to help a visually impaired elementary school student with his schoolwork.

In 1991, my beloved mom passed away, and in her memory, I created a Save Our Earth creative writing competition for elementary school students. Mom loved nature and made all sorts of arrangements with miniature flora and fauna. I was also passionate about protecting our environment.

Three winning storytellers whose pieces were relevant to "cleaning up our inner and outer environments" received cash awards on Earth Day and were announced in the newsletter of Florida Atlantic University's Pine Jog Center for Environmental Education.

Breath & Visualization Exercise

Close your eyes, if you wish.

Breathe in slowly, one, two, and three, through your nose.
Breathe out slowly one, two, and three, through your mouth.

Inhale slowly one, two, and three.
Exhale slowly one, two, and three.

Now imagine yourself,
thinking of one of your passions.

Visualize yourself fulfilling this passion.

Where are you and what are you doing?
Are you with anyone?
How does it feel?
What does it look like?

And now, when it's time, open your eyes.

How will you create the reality of your passion,
right now, right here?

Planting Seeds for Your Story

Getting to Know You, Your Feelings, Your Emotions, Your Thoughts

1. Select one poem that resonates or connects with your heart and soul.
2. Ask yourself:

    - Why did I select this poem?
    - What does it remind me of? What happened? What feelings arose?
    - Who was involved?
    - Where did this occur?
    - When did it happen?

3. Express your story in any format by writing a poem, essay, play, novel, or lyrics to a song, sketching, drawing, photographing, or making a video.

    - Who were you in the past?
    - Who did you become?
    - Who are you today?
    - Did anyone or anything have an impact or influence on you that might have contributed to who you were, became, or are today?
    - How can you use your story for social change?

4. Did you discover any new revelations from telling your story? Did it resolve any issues? Did you share it with another?
5. How did you feel upon completing your story? Write for three pages, without stopping, without any concern for spelling or grammar.

PART THREE:
Who I Am Today
(Loving Me Is Loving You)

Chapter Five: Passion with Purpose

"I'm Somebody & So Are You." Collage by Vera Hirschhorn.

Introduction:
Man's Search for Meaning,[13]
Discovering Our Passion with Purpose

I DISCOVERED MY "Passion with Purpose" upon the passing of my beloved parents who were Holocaust survivors. My parents lost twenty-two members of their family—their parents, siblings, nieces, and nephews—in Auschwitz and other camps. My dad survived three years in slave labor camps and the Budapest Ghetto.[14] My mom survived the Budapest Ghetto. My uncle survived Bergen Belsen, and my aunt, Auschwitz.

My background taught me that hatred in all its forms can escalate into bullying and eventual violence and genocide as it was during the Nazi regime. Hateful acts were perpetuated by many of the youth movements in pre-war Germany, in spite of some peaceful ones such as The White Rose, led by siblings Hans and Sophie Scholl and others at the University of Munich.

Education became my passion and priority, and I believed that literacy and character education were the solution to all problems. I became aware before, during, and after the Columbine High School shootings, that the tragedy was due to bullying. On a personal note, it pained me greatly to witness my dad's frustrations at being bullied and disrespected for his weaknesses rather than respected for his strengths, talents, and skills. I realize now that my love and empathy for Dad was my "tipping point" that triggered my "passion with purpose."

The Columbine perpetrators who were bullied and then became bullies themselves definitely wanted respect; in fact, they stated in a video a week before the tragic shooting: "Maybe next week we'll get the respect we deserve."

As an educator, I wanted to create programs to prevent bullying and promote self-kindness and self-respect as well as kindness and respect towards others. I wanted to help transform bullies into benevolent beings and victims into victors.

Thus, I founded America's Young Heroes Educational Outreach with projects and resources that were intended to encourage teachers to motivate students to "be the change they wanted to see in the world." My intention was to emphasize the importance of character attributes for their benefit and the benefit of others.

I wanted to inspire students to identify their talents, skills, and interests so as to apply them when faced with challenges; also, I wanted to empower them to triumph over adversities by choosing positive attitudes, positive choices, and positive action to resolve their challenges, whether mental, emotional, and/or physical.

I wanted to help students understand that they have the freedom to choose to change not only their attitude but to choose to change a situation and be part of the solution rather than the problem.

In essence, *I wanted them to learn to love themselves and others.*

How Can You Discover Your "Passion with Purpose"?

THINK OF ONE event, one person, one idea, one decision that has been a trigger, a catalyst for change, positive or negative in your life.

1. Think about your uniqueness, your talents, hobbies, interests; your strengths.
2. Think about issues that bother you at school, community or work and ask yourself: *How can I use my talents & character attributes for the betterment of myself and/or others?*
3. Think about your character attributes: Are you compassionate, caring, loyal, tolerant, understanding, patient, courageous? What can you do with your uniqueness and positive character attributes to improve your life or another's in a meaningful way?
4. Think about your role models, past or present, real or fictional, such as characters in books who inspired you.
5. Think about your experiences or someone else's that you witnessed in childhood or adulthood that might have been painful or enjoyable.

Bullying Awareness

I WAS NEVER bullied in my childhood, adolescence, nor during my college years; at least, I didn't think so. A recent flashback to my junior year abroad, as an exchange student, reminded me of one of the Spanish students at the University of Granada in Spain. I remembered that he asked each time he saw me if the pendant on my necklace was a monkey; my pendant was a *chai*, the Hebrew symbol for the letter 18 and for "life." Not thinking anything of his interpretation, I smiled each time he expressed his curiosity.

Today, I ask myself why I didn't just explain the meaning since he seemed to be innocently ignorant of such symbols in the Jewish faith. I could have used the first time as a teachable moment; instead, I let it go. Then, towards the end of the year, upon studying for our final exam in our arts/architecture course, we were reviewing symbols of the Catholic faith, such as the fish. This often appeared in the architecture of the many churches we visited, and I was ignorant of its meaning. When asked if I was Catholic or Protestant and I replied that I was of the Jewish faith, he walked away and chose to never study with me again.

Is this an example of a subtle form of bullying, or simply an example of ignorance or intolerance and prejudice?

Subtle bullying may not be as easy to spot as outright name-calling or physical aggression, but it can be just as upsetting and isolating. Subtle bullying may lead to being excluded from group activities on purpose. In my case, it was only one individual who excluded me from his life. Thankfully, I had other friends who accepted me for who I was; in fact, I was selected as Miss Foreigner (*Señorita Extranjera*) by the Spanish students I had met in my university classes, and musicians celebrated the event by entertaining me under my balcony with traditional Spanish songs. I still have the blue ribbon.

Lessons learned:

- Our Inaction leads to Action upon us by others.
- We can make an uncomfortable situation a teachable moment.
- We need to be grateful for the people who we do have in our lives rather than focus on those that don't support or accept us for who we are.
- We can feel empathy for the bully.
- Emotional alienation at home can create bullies; according to Deborah Prothrow-Stith, professor of public health at Harvard: "A lot of kids have grief, loss, pain, and it's unresolved."

Traveling Within

Chatter everywhere
beckons me to
travel on empty
and visit within;
Listening in stillness,
from the voice within.

Truth Became My Teacher

The daggers of harsh words
struck my heart like a sword.

The clawing lion's shrieking roar and
snarling threats were blown away by the sudden whirlwind
which crushed and buried them away.

The curse had transmuted into a blessing.
Truth became my teacher.

Transformation

You ask if I had rage?
Inferno within?
I reflect on Dad's nightmares and Mom's tears.

Suddenly, I "witness"
the ghosts in my childhood:
My grandparents, aunts, uncles, and cousins
In the embers and smoke of Auschwitz and other camps.

Yet light emanates from many lamps:
Friendships, Queens College, and University of Granada,
colleagues, marriage, children, teaching respect, my Young
Heroes programs, and books.

I face my demons as I revisit my birthplace and soon,
Vinegar transforms into Honey;
Fears transform into Love;
Pain transforms into Passion;
Passion transforms into Purpose!

Transitions

In yesteryears, I spoke:
Loudly, for the downtrodden,
Angrily, for the persecuted victims of bigoted despots
Volcanically, for the environment, abused by pesticides,
Explosively, for preventive medicine!

I spoke at conferences, seminars, and convocations.

I spoke to convince,
I spoke to persuade.

I'm right, don't you see?

Ego was my Muse,
Turmoil was my Inspiration!

Today, I prefer to speak:
softly,
happily,
passionately,
lovingly.

I speak at conferences, seminars, and workshops.

I speak to praise:
My young heroes;
My teen rescuers;
My adolescent volunteers.

I speak to applaud:
Their heroic friendships;
Their patriotism;
Their compassion and caring;
Their self respect and respect for others;

Their positive attitude to overcome fears and other challenges!

They're right, don't you see?
Heart is their Muse
Heroism is their Inspiration!

"Who Am I?"

I am the one who is nourished with the colorful palette of
music, poetry, and dance;
I am the one who thrives on love like the inseparable mallard,
its mate, and family.

Or the monarch who's attracted to milkweed and transforms
from caterpillar to butterfly.
Like the hummingbird, nurtured by the sweet nectar
of lilies and lupines.

I am the one who is grateful to flora and fauna like the turtle
who's taught me to slow down.

I am the one who lives life with passion and purpose:
Celebrating victorious parents of genocide
And teens who are heroes, too!
Telling their story of triumph over tragedy
Unlike my four young cousins who perished, due
to hatred and bigotry.

I am the one who gave a VOICE to teens
To prevent bullying and promote respect through the arts.

I am the one who believes in new beginnings.
I am the one for change!

I Am...

In my youth I lived in the shadows of *my* Truth.

I needed to re-discover who *I am*

And return to *my essence!*[15]

I'm Somebody & So Are You![16]

Let's revere our differences and exalt our likenesses;
Let's strive for oneness.

Let's embrace with grace,
Our imperfections and our perfections.

Let's share our fears and our pain
As they dissolve down memory lane.
And let's celebrate the victories in our histories.

Let's revere our differences and exalt our likenesses;
Let's strive for oneness.

Let's empathize and harmonize,
Compromise and aggrandize:
The greatness of you and the greatness of me.

Examples of My Passion with Purpose Projects

Spirit of Heroes Competition

To promote self-kindness, self-respect, and kindness and respect towards others in order to prevent bullying

I CREATED THE Daniel & Judith Ripp "Spirit of Heroes" competition in 1999 and all anti-bullying programs in subsequent years because of my family's experience with hatred during the European genocide of the 1940s.

Students and teachers were invited to participate in my "Spirit of Heroes" competition to teach tolerance and understanding. Awards were given to students who wrote stories that demonstrated acceptance and open-mindedness towards another's religion; race; mental, emotional, or physical abilities; socio-economic background; or sexual orientation; or towards naturalized immigrants from different nations.

Employee Focus, a newsletter for staff members of the School District of Palm Beach County, announced the contest in their April 12-16, 1999, issue.

Excerpts of Students' Award-Winning Stories

1. "I live in an Orthodox Jewish Community, and I am Catholic. At Christmas time, I joke that we won the holiday lights contest again. This is easy because we have the only decorated house. It all started when I saw a sign for a Sunday Jewish Soccer League. My dad, being a champ at soccer, said, "Let's go." Even though we're Catholic, they accepted us. My dad became a coach, and I became a member of the team. Now I'm invited to birthday parties and have Jewish Orthodox friends. We have learned to respect and accept each other's religions and customs."

2. "It makes me sad when I see people with one arm or in a wheelchair. I know every parent wishes for a healthy baby, but sometimes it's just not to be. Therefore, everybody should be more understanding of people with a physical disability because with one car hitting you or any other accident, you could be one of those people who are now disabled in some way."

3. "Human beings come in all shapes as well as sizes. There's tall, small, thin, fat, black, white, red, and yellow people. We are all of the human race, all brothers and sisters, and to live in harmony one must learn to respect and tolerate all people in one's life, no matter how hard it may seem."

4. "So many people who created new inventions or contributed towards positive changes in the world have been immigrants."

America's Young Heroes Contests and Programs

As a result of the tragic shooting at Columbine High School in Colorado in 1999 by Eric D. Harris and Dylan B. Klebold, the mission of the annual America's Young Heroes programs and contests emphasized the need to prevent bullying and promote respect. Teachers of all disciplines implemented the programs in their lesson plans.

Essays, poetry, and art, as well as thought-provoking questions were published in my second book, *America's Young Heroes Journal*. Thanks to Allison Janse, senior editor at Health Communications, Inc., my book received the 2001 first place award for a published juvenile book by the Florida State Association of the National League of American Pen Women.

The following are examples of students' award-winning solutions to bullying in song, short films or videos, stories, poetry, and art.

Song

ANDREA'S SONG, "IT IS NOW," not only describes her pain as a bullied victim in the first stanza, but also progresses to self-empowerment, as her solution, in the last stanza.

It Is Now
Lyrics and melody by Andrea Casanova

Time is running out,
As the truth lies behind the smiles
All the cries are getting out,
Enduring the pain all the while.

Pre-Chorus:
Emotionally and physically scarred for life,
You wonder when to take action, now's the time.

Chorus:
With the words they say
And all the games they play,
It is more than just the actions that make the mark.
All the tears have been shed,
Due to the words that they've said.
It's the words that make the impact and hit the heart.

The time passes by, as they tolerate what's ahead.
Playing on repeat what people have said.
The struggle to believe what is truly right.
When they feel like they're in for the fight of their life.

2nd Pre-Chorus:
Emotionally and physically torn with what's at hand.
There's more than this to life, and it's time to take the stand.

Chorus:
With the words they say
And all the games they play,
It is more than just the actions that make the mark.
All the tears have been shed,
Due to the words that they've said.
It's the words that make the impact and hit the heart.

Bridge:
We grow up to coexist with everyone around,
But as we hear what they have to say,
We trap ourselves with doubt.
It's anything but the truth,
We can't listen or rearrange.
In and of ourselves, today's the day to make the change.

Final chorus:
Moments in time pass by,
We're taking back our lives.
We are standing on our own, and never looking back.
Living with no regrets,
Nothing but happiness
We now know who we are, unveiling the man-made mask

Years, Days, Minutes, Seconds to overcome
The time has come, and we have won.

Videos

1. One compassionate and caring classmate, bystander, or friend had intervened, as in the video, "Be a Friend."
2. The bullied student in another video, "Meet Me By the Water Fountain...," had the courage to tell an adult such as a teacher, principal, or counselor and discovered that "one knock on a door opened a new one" for her.
3. The bullied teen went to the school police officer as suggested in a third video, "Always Say No to Bullying."
4. Hailey and Jocelyn's video also depicted how the "victim" decided to become a "victor" when she realized she didn't have to change to fit in and asserted: "I don't need you guys to make me feel popular."
5. Michelle, Hope, and Jessica created their video to show the bully's version of why she "acts as if" she's a bully.
6. Haley and Maddison's public service announcement is a warning to all bullies that "Bullying can Backfire."
7. Jordan dedicated his video to a ten-year-old girl who committed suicide due to bullying; he believes that a bully should be forced to take anger management classes and, in the most extreme scenarios, be imprisoned.
8. Sarah and Alexandra's video shows a "victim" of bullies who chose to become a "victor" through her own self-empowerment.

Stories

IN KAILEN'S STORY, "The Strongest Effect," Meghan, Kenneth's victim, had a choice: to believe Kenneth's hurtful words, like "fat" and "geek," which rendered her insecure and insignificant, or believe her friend's encouraging words and suggested solution. She chose an attitude of gratitude over an attitude of self-defeat.

Yasmine, in her story, "Speak Out," told her mom and school dean about being bullied for wearing a hijab and insisted that they promise to let her take care of the situation herself unless the state of affairs became too big of a problem for her to handle. She sat down with the bullies and explained how they made her feel and why she wears the hijab and how much pride she has for her religion, the hijab, and herself. The bullies apologized to her and became her friends and protected her. Yasmine wrote in "Speak Out," that "positive actions make positive reactions; negative actions cause negative reactions," and as sociologist Robert Faris discovered in his recent study, "behavior is contagious."

Olivia wrote about Johnny's courageous choice to assert himself after being cyberbullied and bullied physically and emotionally for many years: "Stop! Okay? Why are you doing this to me? I don't like getting beat up; you guys might find it fun, so punch a pillow or something. But stop punching me. I'm done with it! I don't know why you have the need to bully me. What did I ever do to you? I've actually been thinking about killing myself because of all of you! Please stop!" By expressing his pain, Johnny received apologies from the bullies, who extended their hands to him; they actually became friends, and everyone in the school started being nicer to him!

Poetry

IN HANNAH'S POEM, a popular high school football player, Malcolm, encouraged the "garbage girl," aka the president of the Green Team and lead singer of the band of misfits labeled as "Outcasts," to perform at the spring dance.

Had it not been for Malcolm's recognition and courageous support of the songwriting and musical talents of his peers, they would have continued to be victimized as "Orc-Dorks," "creepy Goths," and "total nerds" rather than applauded and well received by the student body.

GARBAGE GIRL NO MORE!

When I open the locker door, everything falls from within;
Textbooks, binders, folders...
And dead rotting leaves, because someone's broken in.
I hunch my narrow shoulders.

I hear familiar raucous laughter from behind.
Yesterday THEY dumped stale popcorn
And before that, it was watermelon rinds.
"Hey, Green Girl! Why so forlorn?"

This second voice is also familiar, but it is welcomed.
"You mean 'Garbage Girl!'" one of THEM says.
"No, I meant 'Green Girl,'" states Malcolm.
With one last "Buzz off," he leads me away.

Malcolm is popular; he's on the football team.
I'm president of the Green Team...not so cool.
We're social opposites, as school gossip deems.
But I've known him since before preschool.

The walk towards our homes is uneventful,
and we stop at the usual place,
A small park where our words need not be careful
and we say things to each other's face.

I say we need more green awareness.
He thinks we need more sugar at lunch.
I laugh, "Come on! For once, be serious!"
"Um… isn't the spring dance in a time crunch?"

"It's true, the spring dance needs music."
He looks at me, and I know what he's thinking
And I don't like it.
"I don't think that particular group is interested in playing."

And I really do doubt they will want to play.
I am the lead singer of the band he has in mind,
A band of misfits, outcast into labeled clichés,
and to Outcasts, few high schoolers are kind.

But Malcolm convinces me to talk to them,
to see if they'll play at the dance.
I agree only because I know the outcome:
Zero to negative three chance.

As the first students trickle in,
my stomach caught butterflies.
I look at the rest of my band,
to see if they, too, are asking whys.

Why are we here, when we know this arrangement won't work?
The student body detests us; at best we are ignored.
Our violinist and cellist are termed "Orc-Dorks."
A "creepy Goth" plays the keyboard.

Playing guitar is a "total nerd,"
and at the mic is "Garbage Girl."
A plethora of mean words, yet at a word,
we're forced to give our first song a whirl.

And for some reason, no one boos or jeers.
After four or five songs, my cautious cool thaws.
These songs seem to be well received by our peers.
By the end of the night, we're getting hearty applause.

Our songs—original songs—were accepted.
The songs weren't even traditional.
There were no sappy love songs, instead
t'was what misfits think and feel.

The next day, I prepare for the inevitable,
a return to the bottom of the heap,
But suddenly the Outcasts and their clichés as well,
have made a social leap.

No more stuck-out feet in the hallway.
Gone are the nasty remarks.
We've finally found a niche. In our own way
we've learned to make a mark.

Educational Resources

A Journal for You

Hi! I'm Vinnie. I was 17 when I did this sculpture of President Lincoln.

Hi! I'm Elisha. I enlisted as a Volunteer and fought in the Battle of Shiloh. I was 16.

Hi! I'm Susie. I was born a slave. I volunteered to teach and nurse the black soldiers. I was 14.

A JOURNAL FOR YOU
LEARN ABOUT YOURSELF
LEARN THE LESSONS OF THE CIVIL WAR

Book cover by Vera Ripp Hirschhorn.

THIS BOOK IS devoted to the biographies of young heroes of the Civil War such as Vinnie Ream, Elisha Stockwell, Jr., and Susie Baker King Taylor. The second half of the book is an interactive journal of activities for students. Copies were sold at the Shiloh National Military Park, to educators at annual Teachers' Guild conferences, and at book signings at Barnes & Noble in Boca Raton, Florida.

Teens Are Heroes, Too!

Book cover by Natalie Sharp,
art teacher in Palm Beach County.

STORIES OF TRIUMPH over adversity by, for, and about students as well as "hero activities" that included self and peer assessment were published in *Teens Are Heroes, Too! Challenges, Choices and Character.*

The young heroes in the anthology chose to see the essential traits, features, and potential in either themselves, others, or historical teens; in so doing, they were able to transform their sadness, pain, and/or tragedy or those of another into action for their well-being or the well-being of others. They began to discover their "meaning in life" by doing a deed, creating a work, loving a cause, or experiencing or encountering something or someone's goodness, truth, and/or beauty.

This anthology helped students identify their talents, strengths, character attributes, and passions with activities such as "The Peer Identification Questionnaire," "My Hero Checklist," "Talents/Skills Survey," "Hobbies/Interests Survey," "What's Bugging

You?" and "Questions to Think About." In the process, students developed increased self-esteem, self-respect, and respect for each other's diversities. Excerpts are available on YouTube.

Teens Are Heroes, Too! received the first place award for Adult and Young Adult Nonfiction from the Florida State Association of the National League of American Pen Women and the President's Book Award for Best Young Adult Nonfiction from the Florida Authors and Publishers Association.

One of the poems written by 7th grader Lori, "The Right Color of Life: A Tribute to Ruby Bridges," described her hero. Here is an excerpt:

> Once there was an ordinary child,
> Whose family dreamt that she have an education.
> But at the time there was desegregation,
> Which was the norm for our nation.
>
> Therefore, her beginnings
> Were not without strife.
> Because the child came
> From the "wrong" color of life.
>
> Ruby Bridges was just six years old
> When she first entered school.
> The U.S. Marshals had to drive her there
> Because all the white families were so cruel.
>
> Ruby never cried, and never whimpered
> When being attacked or made fun of.
> She relied on her family and the neighbors
> And survived on their support and love.

I'm Somebody & So Are You!

Front cover image from original collage by Vera Ripp Hirschhorn.
Original cover photography by GarrinEvanStudios
and cover design by Gary A. Rosenberg.

MY AWARD-WINNING BOOK, *I'm Somebody & So Are You! The Human Connection in Education* included curricula for college of education students. I had the greatest honor and pleasure collaborating with Dr. Susannah Brown, arts professor at Florida Atlantic University's College of Education, who gratefully implemented the America's Young Heroes curriculum. The creative future teachers produced numerous art exhibits such as "Art with Heart" and "Art Has Character…Images of how Visual Art Supports Positive Interaction for the Betterment of Others" at the College of Nursing.

The goal of the pilot program was to inspire future teachers on an evolutionary journey of self-exploration of strengths, talents, heroic attributes and passion with purpose. Encouraged to collaborate and contribute their art pieces into one single, large collage with teams of other students, all experienced respect for each other's diversities. Thus "separateness" was transformed into "oneness."

Examples of Official Proclamations and Honors

I WAS HONORED to receive accolades from former U.S. Congressman Ted Deutch, who spoke to his fellow Congressmen about my anti-bullying campaign in Palm Beach County schools. His speech was recorded in the Congressional records in 2011.

Congressional Record

PROCEEDINGS AND DEBATES OF THE *112th* CONGRESS, FIRST SESSION

Tuesday, May 31, 2011

House of Representatives

Mr. Speaker,

I rise today to recognize the twenty-six students from Florida schools that have been named winners in the America's Young Heroes contest to promote respect and prevent bullying. These students have admirably put forth concrete, practical, and creative solutions to prevent bullying in America's schools. However, even more important than the proposals is the contest's climate of acceptance and respect that is being spread to schools across Florida through the America's Young Heroes Program.

Founded by Vera Hirschhorn, the America's Young Heroes contest was created in 1999 to improve student's self-esteem through the submission of original stories, poems, music, short films, and artwork about their experiences with bullying. The America's Young Heroes contest has dedicated itself to remedying the bullying epidemic facing our schools by placing an emphasis on positive thoughts and actions to solve bullying situations.

I congratulate Vera Hirschhorn, the America's Young Heroes contest, and the twenty-six Florida students for their great work to end bullying in our schools. Their great work and advocacy on behalf of respect and acceptance is truly making Florida schools a safer place for our children.

TED DEUTCH
Member of Congress

Congressional record of Vera's recognition, 2011.

Scholarships

I CREATED AN arts scholarship titled "I'm Somebody & So Are You" for current and future K-12 teachers and mental health counselors. They were asked to originate curricula and interactive lesson plans to promote self-kindness and kindness towards others at home, school, and community, and to prevent bullying and all forms of intolerance and hatred, such as antisemitism and racism. This scholarship has been given annually to one of thirty-five participating North Carolina teachers each summer at Appalachian State University.

This scholarship is in memory of my beloved parents, Daniel & Judith Friebert Ripp, Holocaust survivors; eternally cherished daughter, Genene; forever missed brother, Hank; and in remembrance of the twenty-two members of my family, including four young cousins—Elvira and Mira Keller Ripp, ages eleven and seven, and Ervin and Eva Friebert, ages eight and six—who perished during the European genocide of the 1940's. It is also in honor of my husband, Martin, and our son, Garrin.

I also created a scholarship with loving tribute to Genene Gila Hirschhorn to keep my daughter alive through the students who receive it. The annual scholarship is for a music therapy student at the University of Miami in the Frost School of Music. These recipients, in turn, help infants, teens, and seniors, like Alzheimer's patients, through music therapy. The scholarship was meant to actualize Genene's passion with purpose and her legacy. Its mission statement is taken from Genene's personal statement in her 2002 application to Berklee College of Music, which follows. The italicized portion is the mission statement of the scholarship.

When I woke up this morning, two songs in a row

came on my alarm clock radio—songs that have a lot of meaning for me and reminded me exactly why I am applying to Berklee College of Music. Whenever "my songs" come on the radio, I take it as a strong sign to listen up—I am receiving a message meant for me.

The first song, "I've Had the Time of My Life," instantly brought me back to the summer after my high school graduation in 1988, upon completing an ecstatic and mesmerizing week of Choral Camp at the University of Miami music school. That song is what me and my fellow camp-goers listened to on someone's boombox in a UM courtyard, as we danced around and celebrated what we had just accomplished in one short week. The song truly captures the energy and spirit I felt there as I pushed my singing abilities all the way to the top, with a caring and supportive staff, and the camaraderie of fellow singers. I recently discovered with surprise in the Berklee prospectus that "I've Had the Time of My Life" was written by Berklee alumni John DiNicola—another prescient sign of how my time at Berklee will be.

The second song on my radio was "Drive" by Incubus. The lyrics of this song are literally one of the major themes of my life—overcoming self-doubt and fear and allowing my true essence and purpose to take the wheel and drive my life. Applying to Berklee is exactly the way I am driving myself back home to my true purpose, which is to sing, and write lyrics and melodies that communicate inspirational messages of insight, catharsis, and comfort to people—in the very same way that a song like "Drive" does for me.

After my UM choral camp experience, I chose to get a bachelor's degree in journalism because of my writing talent, and because I thought I needed a "backup" career for stability and independence. Well, I achieved those things, but my backup became my full-time life instead of my first true love—music. I went from being an honor student and the star singer of my high school in 1988, to my present successful position as the Copy Editor for South Florida's *City Link* magazine, one of the top weekly alternative entertainment publications in the nation. But I have stayed involved in music as much as possible all these years (please see my resume), because my voice and songs never stopped calling me— and now is the time to make the ultimate U-turn to make music my whole life.

On this other path I chose, I had to go through years of insecurity about my identity and purpose in life, to come full circle and realize the only choice in life for me is to be a professional singer and songwriter. *As a granddaughter of two Holocaust survivors, I have personal experience with the pain and struggles of being human. I know I am meant to help people through my voice and songs. As a singer and songwriter, I am in the business of human emotion. Nothing could have prepared me better for this than the past decade of emotional challenges I've faced including anxiety and depression.*

So the type of music I most enjoy listening to, writing, and playing is any music with a deep inspirational message, because I am a messenger myself. I am a voice of comfort and insight—but most of all, emotion. Every time I have ever performed for people, they have been profoundly touched. My audiences over the years always enjoyed what I shared and believed in me. I just needed time to learn to believe in myself. Now I do, and that is why I am here applying to Berklee. It's time to cultivate and share what

I've been given to create joy for myself and others, the same way my favorite artists have done for me.

I've enclosed several audio and lyric samples of music I've written and recently performed at City Link Music Festival. Also enclosed is my audio solo improv performance of "There Comes a Time to Be Thankful" on Gusman Hall stage at UM during that magical summer. Additionally, a video shows my powerful rendition of the national anthem for a live audience of three thousand people, as well as a touching "Sunrise, Sunset" for a wedding. They are all a good indication of what type of music I enjoy. I am thankful for the opportunity to share my voice and message with all of you at Berklee, and I excitedly await my arrival in Boston come September.

Breath & Visualization Exercise

Let's close our eyes for a brief relaxation exercise

Let's breathe *out* tension and tightness,
And breathe *in* relaxation and resilience.

Let's breathe *out* all fears & anxieties,
And breathe *in* fortitude & strength.

Let's breathe *out* all self-judgements
And breathe *in* self-acceptance just the way we are.

Now imagine fulfilling your heart-felt passion
with purpose project.

Visualize your project.

How does it feel to do this for your well-being?
How will you share it for the betterment of others?

And when you are ready, open your eyes gently and actualize your passion with a purpose project.

Planting Seeds for Your Story

Getting to Know You, Your Feelings, Your Emotions, Your Thoughts

1. Select one poem that resonates or connects with your heart and soul.
2. Ask yourself:

    - Why did I select this poem?
    - What does it remind me of? What happened? What feelings arose?
    - Who was involved?
    - Where did this occur?
    - When did it happen?

3. Express your story in any format by writing a poem, essay, play, novel, or lyrics to a song, sketching, drawing, photographing, or making a video.

    - Who were you in the past?
    - Who did you become?
    - Who are you today?
    - Did anyone or anything have an impact or influence on you that might have contributed to who you were, became, or are today?
    - How can you use your story for social change?

4. Did you discover any new revelations from telling your story? Did it resolve any issues? Did you share it with another?
5. How did you feel upon completing your story? Write for three pages, without stopping, without any concern for spelling or grammar.

Chapter Six:
Spiritual Awakenings

Surviving the COVID-19 Pandemic. Collage by Vera Hirschhorn.

Introduction

*It is said that democracy or freedom is obtained when
we can look at sad, hurtful, or terrible memories objectively,
as an observer or a witness, without judgments or analysis,
so that we can move forward and grow.*
(My translation from a document seen at the
Conciergerie in Paris, France)

WHAT HAS THE School of Life taught me? It has taught me that sometimes I'll experience storms in my personal, social, professional, or spiritual life and other times, peace. The question is what do I do when the storm arises? Will I respond or react? It's all up to me because I have free will to choose my wants and attitude. Do I want to be angry and miserable, or do I want to be happy and joyful?

At this stage of my life, I want to view my past or present stormy challenges as honeyed blessings. I want to view and act upon past mistakes as lessons to grow from without guilt or regret. All I want is to give and receive love. I want to forgive and be forgiven.

Before the coronavirus pandemic, I wanted to elevate my mood at the beginning of each day and help others do the same, especially teachers, parents, and students. As an educator who had been invited to present workshops for future teachers relevant to teaching tools from my book, *I'm Somebody & So Are You!,* I shared my daily morning rituals in which I asked myself, "What joy will I give myself today? What joy will I give another? How will I love myself today and share the love with others?" I told them that my day was generally filled with much more light, love, and laughter.

During the COVID crisis, the human connection was needed for all of us more than ever, and thus, I prepared a blog and video for educators and parents titled "Healing with Coping Skills," which included stress-reducing techniques such as:

I. Deep Breathing, followed by mindfulness and visualization
II. Boosting one's mood in the morning with

    a. Gratitude Journaling
    b. Listening/dancing to a favorite musical playlist;
    c. Reading and reciting inspirational affirmations
    d. Engaging in self-love activities.

III. Transforming Negative Self-Talk into Positive Self-Talk, thereby moving from victim to victor. ("I/he must, I demand, or I should! It's awful, horrible! I can't stand it!" becomes "I prefer, I wish. It's unfortunate. I don't like it, but I can stand it & handle it.")
IV. Exploring *Who You Are* through introspection and the arts.
V. Focusing on solutions rather than on problems.
VI. Volunteering and mentoring (from a distance) to discover one's passion and act upon one's purpose in life.

There's Light across the Lake

There's light across the lake
And there's darkness here;
The lake reflects the light
And there's gloom right here.

There's hope across the lake.
There's despair here in the shadows!
Where are the green, green meadows?

There's light across the lake
Persistent, almost obsessive;
When will it reach here?
Can I create it?

In My Solitude

During COVID-19

I, LIKE EVERYONE else, was clueless as to what was happening.

In my solitude, I yearned to breathe in the ocean air and be mesmerized and hypnotized by the sounds of the foamy ocean waves for inner peace and inspiration. And one day, I decided to take a major step. Armed with my mask, I drove A1A to the Red Reef Park in Boca Raton and walked on the boardwalk. Freedom was going to the ocean, which became my sanctuary; the waves became my friends who welcomed me unconditionally with wide open arms. I enjoyed our dialogues, big and small. The ocean became my muse.

The granulated particles of shells and rocks also welcomed me as my toes sank into an abyss of warmth and comfort and cradled me firmly in soothing reverie. No need to be perfect here. No need to fear!

Vera during the pandemic. Photo by Marty Hirschhorn.

Oh, Lights of My Sabbath

How you calm
How you beckon me to slow down

Oh lights of my Sabbath

I honor your golden reflection
I embrace this sacred time with you alone.

Just you and me
Like lovers warming each other's hearts
Like lovers reaching out for each other's light

Nowadays

The streets are empty,
the frenzy is gone.

I lament your absence
and await your presence.
What's certain is impermanence,
and the existence of the sea.

I survived the storm,
outside and within.
Patience, I'm practicing;
Gratitude, I'm feeling.

This very moment, I'm enjoying;
Yesterday, I'm forgiving;
The future, no longer fearing!

Hoy Dia

Las calles están vacías,
Y la gente desaparecida.

Lamento tu ausencia,
Espero tu presencia.
Lo que es cierto es la impermanencia,
Y la existencia del mar.

Sobreviví la tormenta,
De afuera y de adentro;
Paciencia aprendí,
El amor me siento.

Gozo de este momento,
Perdono el pasado;
No temo el futuro,
Y agradezco
Lo que tengo.

In Storms

In storms I want to be grounded like the palm trees,
bending in the wind;
yet still standing.

I want to be graced with white orchids,
peaceful and calm;
and inhale
white gardenias as they
soothe and balm.

I want to sleep in the moonlight's shadows
like blooming purple showers
that awaken as the sun rises.

I want to be in my garden amidst my rainbow of flowers.
I want to return to a place
where love reigns
and hate evaporates into clouds.

I want to return to a place
where showers of rainbows
cleanse and paint us as
ONE.

I want to return to a place
where the kaleidoscope of butterflies fly freely
and birds sing in my garden of gardenias,
IN HARMONY.

I want to return to a place
where we share each other's stories,
feel each other's pain
and celebrate each other's joy,
TOGETHER!

Friendships

HAIKU

Flowers like Friendships,
Endure heavy springtime rains
And grow, regardless!

Friendships

*Dedicated to all my special friends for whom I'm so grateful.
You mean so much to me!*

It's not the number of times we've been together,
Nor the number of years.

It's the times we've talked and laughed amidst occasional tears.
It's the times we've shared and experienced joy amidst sorrow.

It's the times we've metamorphosized,
accepting the past and together,
looking forward to our tomorrows.

I Am a Bubble[17]

Sometimes I easily burst. Other times, not.
I can linger around and just float into space, without direction
Or I can land heavily and drop onto someone for anchorage.

One very special bubble, strong and firm, showed me the light
to persevere and to hang in there.
I felt love and confidence to move on.

I'm flying and enjoy floating with other bubbles.
Exploring new horizons, new adventures.

I can be colorful with tinges and hues of reds, pinks, blues;
Transparent, translucent, opaque.
I don't mind being transparent, for I like to be sociable.

I'm a happy bubble and living in the now!

Freedom Now

I'm truly free!
I can fly wherever;
Alone, with you, or whomever.
I can move like the clouds,
Or like the tropical wind.
I can reach for the stars
Or reach for my car.

I can dance flamenco, tap dance,
Salsa, foxtrot or Bollywood.
My choices are endless,
In stockings or socks.

I'm blessed with teachers
For body and mind;
How fortunate for me,
They're all so kind.

I'm grateful to friends and family
Who care.
As well as to students
Who truly dare.
They express their hurt, sorrow and pain;
And inspire me
They overcame!

Most of all, I'm proud to be me!
My essence is pure;
My spirit, strong.
I've come home,
Where I belong!

What Is Happiness?

What is happiness?
Is it the sun trying to peek through the dark clouds
on a windy, rainy day of tornados?
Is it an art piece with its message,
"Welcome to my happy home"
When I'm feeling blue?

What is happiness?
Is it my garden blooming with pink starbursts in the winter?
Or my pink & purple orchids drinking
from the pandemus tree,
to which they're attached?

What is happiness?
Is it practicing yoga each morning,
And waking up, gratefully, with pain-free muscles?

What is happiness?
It's what I have when I want it and will it;
It's the light within me and the light within you.
It's living in the present moment.

On My Road to Me

Where are you going?
Where have you been?

I'm on my road to me;
To me, myself, not he.

Entangled like a spider
In the web of others' lives.

Caring for them, speaking for them,
Teaching them.

And Now,
I'm on the road to me
Caring for me!

Taking Care of Me

I behold my personal handheld shower;
And feel the light spray
Awaken my senses.
The soft rain soothes my tense muscles and tendons!

The healing waters caress my skin,
And kiss my private parts.
My soul has been enlightened,
And I've begun to seize the day.

Clearly I See

My Inner Child beckons once again
To see clearly what I've resisted to see.
What my soul craves,
What wisdom has taught,

What my heart has sought.

Surrender to what is;
Forget what was;
Love is Now,
Now is Love.

My Inner Child beckons once again
To see the greatness in me
The greatness in You
To trust me and to trust You.

My eyes beckon once again
To play,
To laugh,
To paint with words:

The power of love
The feeling of love
The essence of love
The freeing of love.

The power of love is mightier than the love of power!

I Celebrate…

I celebrate her gray hair,
Her wrinkles,
Her bitten nails, her teeth,
Her aging.

I celebrate her anxieties,
Her ego,
Her soul,
Her faith.

I celebrate her Brooklyn accent,
Her smiles,
Her grace,
Her gait.

I celebrate her dance,
Her art,
Her books,
Her poems,
Her guitar, her voice.

I celebrate her mate,
Her kids…her own and at school

I celebrate her country, her heritage
Her community, her home.

I celebrate her compassion,
Her independence,
Her dignity,
Her self-respect.
I CELEBRATE ME!

My Harmonious Heart

I may not be able to control
the disharmony in this world.
I may not be able to stop the rise in hate.
I may not be able to halt what others think, feel, or do.

What can I do?

I can feel harmony
within me, through me;
above, below, and around me.

I can call, walk, talk, feel with you.
I can listen with an open heart.

My harmonious heart!

Mi Corazón Armonioso

No puedo detener
la discordia en el mundo,
ni parar el odio creciente;
ni controlar
lo que piensas, o dices, o haces, o lo que te sientes.

Pero puedo,
llamarte;
sentir lo que sientes;
andar y hablar contigo
y escucharte
con todo mi ser,
con todo mi Corazón!

Mi Corazón Armonioso.

A Path to Paradise

I wish only a path of love;
And if by chance, I stumble on rocks,
May they become pebbles
With insights from above.

Let's ascend towards the light
And transcend any darkness.
Let's renew and refresh
like the perfumed perennials
year after year.

So walk with me,
share with me,
laugh with me,
celebrate with me!

Let our spirits soar
and our loving souls explore
PARADISE,

TOGETHER!

Un Camino de Amor

Deseo para mí un camino de amor
Y si a lo largo, me tropiezo con piedras,
Ojalá que lleguen a ser guijarritos
Con verdades desde arriba

Vamos hacia la luz
Y dejamos el pasado.
Vamos a renacer
como las flores perfumadas
año tras año.

Pues,camina conmigo,
Comparte conmigo,
Ríe conmigo,
Celebra conmigo!

Ojalá que nuestros espíritus se eleven;
Y nuestras almas llenas de amor
exploren
EL PARAISO

JUNTOS!

What Is Life?

What is life?
It's a baby's first breath
from the depths of darkness
to its mother's first warm embrace.

What is life?
It's discovering our soul's purpose
from the depths of darkness
to newly found feelings of love for self and others.

What is life?
It's the rising of the sun
from the depths of darkness,
to the glistening, ever-changing sea.

What is life?
It's the awakening of purple showers
from the depths of darkness
to blessing us with their beauty.

And what is death?
It's our last breath;
transforming into the eternal light
and our never-ending cycles of life.

"Going Home"[18]

*Dedicated to my mother-in-law, Bertha Hirschhorn,
who "went home" on July 23, 2014, at age ninety-eight*

In the haze of her clouds,
She repeated in short breaths:
"I want to go home."
"I want to go home."

Home, where was home?
Only she knew, and she was ready.

Drifting in and out of the fog
She repeated almost breathless:
"I want to go home."

"Mom, it's time to forgive all those who pained you
In your yesterdays and yesteryears.
It's time!
It's time to surrender!"

Ears listened to their last words;
Eyes opened to his tender touch
And final kiss.

Suddenly, she was at peace.

With rainbows of her life,
The sweet gentle spirit
Returned home.

Loving Me Is Loving You

For so, so long, I cared about others:
My parents, brother, husband, my two gems, my young heroes.
Along the way,
I lost myself.

Fear overwhelmed me;
Weakness ensued.
Emotionally drained,
I was forced into stillness.

My soul needed love.

Little by little, moments of stillness brought forth
expressions of love through poems, drawings, paintings
of furry monkeys, birds with crystal beads for
eyes, flowers and trees.
They cheered me, they enlivened my soul.

Collages of my music, my garden and the ocean
Proudly hung in my den;
Transforming my pain into passion with action.

Day by day, the light within began to glow
like my Sabbath candles;
And my soul whispered,
Love Yourself! Be kind to Yourself!
Nurture, nourish You!

Healing takes one day at a time:

Releasing fears;
Sharpening my senses;
Seeing Life's Luminescence.

I Followed the Light
Drinking from my Source,
I let go of remorse.

Light overpowered Darkness;
No room for Discord.
Light healed my wounds.

I Opened my Heart,
And Love entered,
Self-love and love for others.

Loving me is loving you!

Breath & Visualization Exercise

Close your eyes if you wish and
Place your right hand on your belly.

Breathe in relaxation through your nose,
one, two, three.
Now slowly, breathe out stress and strain through your mouth
one, two, three.

Inhale love and light
Exhale sadness and darkness.

Now, envision yourself in your "happy place."
Where are you?

And ask yourself:

> How will I love, nurture and nourish myself today?
> How will I share my love in my personal, social, professional and/or financial life?

Planting Seeds for Your Story

Getting to Know You, Your Feelings, Your Emotions, Your Thoughts

1. Select one poem that resonates or connects with your heart and soul.
2. Ask yourself:

    - Why did I select this poem?
    - What does it remind me of? What happened? What feelings arose?
    - Who was involved?
    - Where did this occur?
    - When did it happen?

3. Express your story in any format by writing a poem, essay, play, novel, or lyrics to a song, sketching, drawing, photographing, or making a video.

    - Who were you in the past?
    - Who did you become?
    - Who are you today?
    - Did anyone or anything have an impact or influence on you that might have contributed to who you were, became, or are today?
    - How can you use your story for social change?

4. Did you discover any new revelations from telling your story? Did it resolve any issues? Did you share it with another?
5. How did you feel upon completing your story? Write for three pages, without stopping, without any concern for spelling or grammar.

Heartfelt Gratitude to Family, Friends, and Colleagues:

MARTY FOR YOUR endless love and support during the highs and lows of our life together. You were always there, by my side, during the highlights of my professional projects. And thank you, my hubby, for the yummy lunches or dinners you brought home while I was editing with Jessica.

Garrin, I've always enjoyed our enlightening phone conversations. You've been my light and inspiration in so many ways. Loving you has always been easy.

And you always believed in my America's Young Heroes project. I still have one of your emails praising my work: "Mom, this is really fantastic what you're doing! I watched the videos. I especially like the documentary and 2nd place cinematic winners. It brings back memories of my recycling rap PSA video (remember how we won 1st place statewide?)." How surprised I was to learn that you nominated me for CNN's *Heroes* awards!

Genene, I'll always cherish our hugs and our times of laughter. I love you forever. I never realized how much we had in common, especially poetry! I tried theatre; you were the pro; I tried singing; you were the pro. I was amazed when you appeared, unannounced, at my America's Young Heroes awards ceremonies for students and teachers. And how pleasantly surprised I was when you recorded my fun story on NPR radio during their Sunday storytelling segment.

Maureen, your magical hands creating crafts to brighten my world; your support and love, along with that of my nieces and nephew, whether during professional events or during the toughest times in our life, especially during the loss of my beloved Genene and our loss of our beloved Hankie, will never be forgotten.

Doris and my nephews, who shared fun and loving stories of Genene that I read to her while she was still with us. Doris, your warmth, companionship, and loving help after the memorial and while we were sitting Shiva will always be remembered.

Mira, aka. Miritza, my precious cousin who I've literally known since the early days of our birthplace and our challenging travels from Europe to the United States. As 2-Gs, I always enjoy reliving our family' s stories. Look how far we've come! More than anything, thank you for always being there for Genene, practically as her second mother, and for me during these last two-plus years. I could always count on your unconditional love and compassion.

Bobby, my deepest gratitude for your being there daily, each time I called you during the recent painful years and acting almost as a therapist. It meant the world to me.

Artie, my sweet, wise, and treasured cousin; I've always adored you for your kindness and helping me learn English during our early days in America. And I'll never forget how you entertained my parents, Hank, and me with your funny imitations of our favorite comic, Jerry Lewis. I was and am still so proud of your talents as record producer for some of the top rock bands in the country. In fact, whenever I hear your bands, I brag to everyone, "That's my Cous Artie!" Steven must have inherited your creativity as he painted the most beautiful painting of Genene for her memorial.

Louie, for the photo of my first home in America and for the heart-to-heart conversations we still have about our back-to-our roots trips to Europe, connecting our Ripp-Berger-Jacob families. Even today, I have your drawing of our genealogies. I love reminiscing with you.

My dearest childhood friends, Barbara and Linda; and my dearest Floridian friend Fran, who introduced herself with her compassionate heart thirty-five years ago. And of course, my puppeteer friend, Wendy. How wonderful to have supported and known each other inside and out through "all kinds of weather"! My N.C. friends, Karen, Gail, Zodie, Sharon, Nancy, Bonnie, Amy Hudnall. It's so wonderful to enjoy all that we do in the cool temps of the High Country during the sizzling hot summers in Florida. (Amy, I can't thank you enough for all you've done to help me with the scholarship for teachers during the symposiums at ASU in Boone.)

My inspirational Pen Women colleagues in the Boca Raton Chapter who have become friends since 2000. Emily Rosen who taught me, "show, don't tell." Marlene, I cherish your continued support and praises for my poetry especially in my memoir. I'm especially grateful to the Florida State Pen Women who have awarded many of my books in state competitions.

Much gratitude to Angela Page, President of the South Florida chapter of the Women's National Book Association; Suzanne Austin-Hill from the Florida State Poetry Association, and especially Ruth Van Alstine.

And my fun, animated Spanish-speaking friends: our beloved Ed, Alene (thanks so much for the review), David, Doris, Leah, and all our other amigos. Muchísimas gracias a todos.

Above all, thanks so much to Lucy at Pen Women Press for believing in this labor of love of mine and making this journey easier than I expected. And Jessica, heartfelt thanks for your patience and enthusiasm in helping me edit "bits and pieces of my life." I always felt so comfortable connecting with you; in fact, I feel as if you've become family. Welcome aboard!

You are all blessings in your own unique ways. I love you all.

About the Author

Photo by Garrin Evan.

VERA RIPP HIRSCHHORN is an educator, educational consultant, workshop presenter for professional development, storyteller for National Public Radio, and award-winning author of five books and poetry, including poems honored by the Poets of the Palm Beaches and the National League of American Pen Women. In 1995, Hirschhorn introduced her original Hero Activities to students in Palm Beach County schools with an emphasis on self-respect and respect for diversity and safe environments in schools and community. She originated the Daniel and Judith Ripp "Spirit of Heroes" Award, a multimedia competition to teach tolerance and understanding in memory of her beloved parents, heroic survivors. In 1999, as her response to the Columbine High School tragedies, she created the America's Young Heroes arts programs, curriculum and educational resources for grades 6-university level to promote kindness, prevent bullying and hatred, and help students increase self-esteem while improving character, reading, writing, and problem-solving skills. For this, Vera received congratulatory accolades from former U.S. Congressman Ted Deutch and the 111th and 112th U.S. Congress, which were recorded in the Congressional Records. She won the Florida Publishers Association President's Award for the Best Young Adult Non-Fiction Book. One of her fondest memories has been to receive awards from the NLAPW at national and state levels. Vera lives in South Florida with her husband.

Endnotes

1. My dad's sister, Aunt Irene, and her two little girls, Elvira and Mira, stood before Mengele, "the angel of death," upon their arrival to Auschwitz, the extermination camp. My Aunt Beba was also with them and had volunteered to take one of the girls with her to the other line, but the girls stayed with their mother. Tragically, Aunt Irene and her two precious girls were forced into the gas chamber since the children were too young to work. Had Aunt Irene permitted a daughter to go to the other line, Aunt Beba would have been killed along with them. Those who were too old, like my paternal grandmother, also were forced into the gas chambers.

2. My dad was sent to the Budapest Ghetto in 1944 as a result of his wounds from three years in slave labor camps. Beginning in March 1944, Jews lived under strict laws, and those who didn't have protective papers from a neutral power were forced into the Ghetto as prisoners by early December 1944. The fascist Arrow Cross, who had dominated the new Hungarian government since October 1944, instituted a reign of terror in Budapest, and hundreds of Jews were shot.

   Between December 1944 and January 1945, the Arrow Cross seized and murdered as many as twenty thousand Jews from the Budapest Ghetto. They hurled their bodies into the Danube River.

In the second week of January 1945, Raul Wallenberg learned that Adolf Eichmann planned to massacre the prisoners of the largest Jewish ghetto in Budapest. General Gerhard Schmidhuber, commander of the German forces in Hungary, was the only man assigned to stop it. Wallenberg threatened the general with being hanged as a war criminal once the war was over if he followed through with the murders. The general knew that the war would soon end and the Germans would lose, so the mass annihilation was stopped at the last minute, thanks to Wallenberg's courage and bold actions.

Soviet forces liberated Budapest on February 13, 1945. More than one hundred thousand Jews remained in the city at liberation.

3   *The Top Five Regrets of the Dying* by Bronnie Ware

4   Bloodstained Danube refers to the Novi Sad (Serbia) Massacre or the Raid (Razzia) in January 1942. This was a military operation carried out by the armed forces, or Kiralyi Honvedseg, of Hungary. More than one thousand Jewish civilians–like my paternal grandfather–and Serbian civilians were shot or thrown and shoved amidst the ice sheets of the Danube waters where they drowned.

The goal of the military and the Hungarian government under Miklos Horthy was to suppress the Partisan resistance and strengthen ties with Nazi Germany. In 1943 the Hungarian government and news media condemned the Raid and conducted a mass trial of the four organizers, all of whom escaped to Germany before the executions. After the war, several trials were held in Hungary and the former Yugoslavia. The final court proceedings took place in 2011 when Sándor Képíró was tried and acquitted of murdering the civilians in Novi Sad, He died six weeks later at age ninety-seven. Until his trial, Képíró was on the Simon Wiesenthal Center's list of one of the most wanted Nazi war criminals.

For more information, see the 2025 documentary *Novi Sad Remembrance*, directed by Aleksandar Reljić, and the 1966 film *Cold Days* (*Hideg napok*), directed by András Kovács, based on the novel of the same name by Tibor Cseres.

5   The Promised Land. The 1948 Arab/Israeli civil war was the second and final stage of the 1948 Palestinian War. It formally began following the end of the British Mandate for Palestine on May 14, 1948. The Israeli Declaration of Independence had been issued earlier that day, and a military coalition of Arab states including Egypt, Transjordan, Syria, and expeditionary forces from Iraq, entered Palestine. The invading forces took control of the Arab areas and immediately attacked Israeli forces and several Jewish settlements. The ten months of fighting took place mostly on the territory of the British Mandate and in the Sinai Peninsula and southern Lebanon. My parents, brother, and I lived in a shack near the Lebanese border in the town of Betzet during these wars, and my Aunt Beba, Uncle Mike, and cousin Mira invited us to live with them in Nahariya until the wars ended in 1949.

6   Unbeknown to Garrin's grandfather, in 1941, after the invasion of Novi Sad (Ujvidek) by the Hungarians, his older brother Imre fled to Budapest. As a member of the youth movement, the Hashomer Hatzair, he took part in the underground activities of the Yugoslav anti-fascist committee; activities included sabotage of military factories and granaries, especially after the razzia, or raid, in January 1942, at which time their father was murdered and thrown

into the icy Danube. Imre was caught and sent to do forced labor in the Ukraine, where he perished. He was posthumously commemorated by the Organization of Partisans, Underground Fighters and Ghetto Rebels in Tel Aviv, Israel.

7 BACKGROUND: Youth Movements in Serbia, Uncle Imre's birthplace

In 1919 the first youth organization was founded by Sarah Sari Cohen (who moved to Jerusalem becoming one of the leaders of the world-wide organization Hadassah).

In 1927 a local Jewish scouting movement called Hashomer (The Guard) was established by a student named Rudolph Freedman. He became a pharmacist and was killed by the Hungarian occupiers in 1941. Freedman's innovation was in the merging of scouting and the love of nature with Jewish nationalist education. In 1931 a chapter of Hashomer Hatzair (The Young Guard) was founded by A. Eckstein, Z. Lokerand, and O. Guttman. Uncle Imre was a member and died for having fought in the Underground Resistance. He was highly praised and honored by the Israeli Organization of Partisans, Underground Fighters and Ghetto Rebels.

8 Hank, you were the best brother a sister could have and a wonderful human being. I love you eternally.

9 This poem won first place in a poetry contest sponsored by the Boca Raton Chapter of National League of American Pen Women.

10 This poem was selected for inclusion in the exhibition, *Fun in the Sun* held at Palm Beach International Airport. The

exhibition was a part of Destination: Culture, an ongoing series of exhibitions underwritten by a donation from HMSHost Corporation.

It was displayed on a 20 x 30 inch board, framed and installed on the Main Concourse of the airport (level 2) along with accompanying artwork. This was a project of the Palm Beach County Art in Public Places. With gratitude to Program Director F. Joan Goldberg.

11 The Sierra Club and the Palm Beach Poets honored me for this poem in their Earth Day celebration.

12 Yo recibí un premio por este poema gracias al Club Sierra y a los Poetas de las Playas de Palm Beach en celebración del Día de la Tierra.

13 Title of Victor Frankl's book

14 The Nazi occupation of Budapest (Operation Margarete) began on March 19, 1944, and the Ghetto was created by decree of the Hungarian Royal Government. The perimeter was surrounded by a high fence reinforced with boards and was strictly guarded to prevent smuggled goods from sneaking in and people from leaving. Seventy thousand Jews were displaced in an area of 0.1 square miles (0.26 square kilometers). Budapest was liberated by Soviet forces during fighting on January 17, 1945. Like other ghettos set up elsewhere in Nazi-occupied Europe, the area was completely cut off from the outside world. No food was allowed to be brought in, garbage and waste were not collected, and the dead were lying on the streets and left unattended. A large amount of supplies piled up in the storefronts that were blown up, causing the buildings to become overcrowded and leading to the spread of

diseases such as typhoid fever. More than half of those interned in the Ghetto in 1944 were sent to concentration camps shortly after the Ghetto was established. Between occupation and liberation, Budapest's Jewish population had dwindled from to hundred thousand to seventy thousand within the Ghetto.

15　It is said that before birth we are given our "essence," our "real" self, our true self. After birth, we forget our "essence" and need to re-discover it; that is, to look within and see who we really are and what our mission is in our new life while learning from our mistakes.

16　The title of this poem was inspired by Emily Dickinson's poem "I'm Nobody! Who are you?" (1891), the antithesis to the underlying theme of my life's work.

17　This poem was featured as the Poem of the Week on the National League of American Pen Women's website for the week of January 7, 2016.

18　This poem was selected Poem of the Week on the blog of the National League of American Pen Women.

www.ingramcontent.com/pod-product-compliance
Lightning Source LLC
Chambersburg PA
CBHW030442090526
44586CB00044B/500